DATE DUE

~~DE2 000~~			

Health and Social Services among International Labor Migrants

CMAS BORDER & MIGRATION STUDIES SERIES
Series Editor: Gilberto Cárdenas

R

Health and Social Services among International Labor Migrants

A Comparative Perspective

edited by
ANTONIO UGALDE & GILBERTO CÁRDENAS

CMAS Books
The Center for Mexican American Studies
The University of Texas at Austin

A CMAS BOOK

Editor: Víctor J. Guerra
Editorial Assistant: Olga L. Mejía

The publication of this book was assisted by a grant from the
Inter-University Program for Latino Research.

Library of Congress Cataloging-in-Publication Data

Health and social services among international labor migrants : a
    comparative perspective / edited by Antonio Ugalde & Gilberto
    Cárdenas. — 1st ed.
        p. cm. — (CMAS border & migration studies series)
    Includes bibliographical references.
    ISBN 0–292–78536–4 (alk. paper)
        1. Transcultural medical care—Europe. 2. Transcultural medical
care—United States. 3. Migrant labor—Medical care—Europe.
4. Migrant labor—Medical care—United States. 5. Immigrants—
Services for—Europe. 6. Immigrants—Services for—United States.
I. Ugalde, Antonio. II. Cárdenas, Gilberto. III. Series.
RA418.5.T73H44 1997
362.1′086′91—dc21   97-31178

♻ ⧜ This book is printed on recycled, acid-free paper that conforms
to the American National Standard of permanence for printed library
materials, as approved by the American National Standards Institute.

Printed and bound in the United States of America.

First edition. First impression, December 1997.

Contents

Introduction

Antonio Ugalde and Gilberto Cárdenas

The articles in this volume represent a selection of papers read at a workshop titled "International Migration: Health and Social Policies" held in Granada, Spain, in May 1995. The workshop was the result of institutional contacts between the International Migration and Human Rights Project of the Center for Mexican American Studies at the University of Texas at Austin and the Andalusian School of Public Health. Faculty from the two institutions saw common concerns and problems in the provision of social and health services to immigrants in the European Union and in the United States. It is understandable that in these days of instant communication and global economics, social problems are also universalized.

Today wealthy nations are engaged in a fierce effort to reduce social spending in the name of economic growth, and the outsiders, the foreigners, the ethnic minorities—many of whom are deprived of political representation—are the first to be deprived of social benefits. Whether political leaders take advantage of the xenophobia to exclude ethnic minorities from basic human services or promote it in order to have a ready excuse to deprive them of the services is a moot question, but in the process many immigrant workers' human rights are violated.

During the preparation of this volume, we have read in the newspapers, heard on the radio, and seen on television the U.S. Congress's debates on whether legal immigrants should or could be denied many social benefits. We also have learned about raids in which undocumented workers are picked up at their workplaces and dropped penniless on the other side of the Rio Grande after their pocket change is taken away by immigration agents in order to compensate for deportation expenses. The raids do not allow these workers to say good-bye to or notify their spouses and children—some of whom are legal residents—of their sudden departure or even to stop at home to pick up a few belongings.

The winds blowing on the other side of the Atlantic are equally somber. There we have learned that tranquilizers have been added to the drinking water of black African immigrants while in custody of security forces to expedite their deportation to Morocco. To reduce deportation costs some member states of the European Union and the government of Morocco have reached an agreement under which Morocco receives and incarcerates deported undocumented Sub-Saharan immigrants. The Moroccan government simply places them in a prison in which the conditions are said to be dismal. At this feared location immigrants have no legal recourse and will stay as long as capricious bureaucrats wish.

The similarities of immigrant experiences on both sides of the Atlantic prompted faculty at the University of Texas International Migration and Human Rights Project and the Andalusian School of Public Health to organize an interdisciplinary workshop on health and policy issues related to international migration. Scholars from the sending societies, including Mexico, Morocco, Egypt, Tunisia, and Turkey, met with colleagues from the United States and several European countries to exchange ideas and to explore solutions to common problems. A total of thirty-five experts from thirteen countries with backgrounds in psychology, sociology, medicine, anthropology, demography, psychiatry, social work, economics, human biology, political science, and public health spent two days in Granada, a city which is itself a crossroads of cultures and civilizations. The interest of the gathering at the Andalusian School of Public Health was the welfare of the international migrant, who frequently has been studied only as a statistic, a factor of production, or a cultural oddity in need of adaptation and integration into the larger society.

What we have selected for this volume does not do justice to the rich exchange of ideas and discussions that took place in Granada and the many personal and institutional linkages that were built in a brief period of time. However, due to economic considerations we had to limit the number of papers we could include. In order to provide some unity to the collection, we have chosen those which were most closely related to the topics of health and human services.

The volume opens with a contribution by Lars Rasmussen, who is the principal administrator of the Public Health Directorate of the European Commission in Luxembourg. Receiving societies frequently are concerned about the diseases imported by immigrants, but Rasmussen reminds us that immigrants should be alerted about the high health risks (such as of heart disease, stroke, and certain types of cancer) that they will be exposed to in the receiving countries as they adopt new lifestyles. One of the many barriers to access to health services is the cultural differences between providers and users of services. To overcome this impediment—an issue that is discussed in several of the articles in this volume—requires political determination and resources. Rasmussen denounces the monoculturalism of European health systems and fears that governments may not respond to the health needs of immigrants because of economic costs. Clearly, the unwillingness to do so would contradict the 1992 European Council recommendation that all legal residents in the Union should have the right to access to health services.

Most labor immigrants come from neighboring countries: in the case of the United States they come mostly from Mexico, the Caribbean, and Central America, and in the European Union they come mainly from the Maghreb and from Eastern Europe. Yolanda Padilla uses the case of the U.S.–Mexico border to document that an effective provision of human services to immigrants requires collaboration between the sending and receiving countries. She discusses the political, economic, and cultural barriers that exist to carry out such collaboration and advances some insightful ideas of what can be accomplished without a major reorganization of social service provisions. As distances between nations have been reduced by increased transportation and lower fares and the demand for cheap labor has continued to grow, we have observed the growth of very large ethnic enclaves in many cities throughout the world and the development of authentic ethnic borders within cities. We would like to suggest that the lessons learned from studies of political borders may have some application in ethnic border areas within countries.

As is the case in the European Union, the U.S. public sector has not been able to provide culturally appropriate health services to immigrants. The New York Task Force on Immigrant Health is a private nonprofit effort that aims at filling the vacuum. Heike Thiel de Bocanegra and Francesca Gany, who work for the task force, describe in their paper the task force's approach to meeting the difficult challenge of offering multicultural health services in one of the most culturally diverse cities in the world. Comparative studies of private organizations are needed if we are going to learn to what extent—in terms of quality, costs, and efficiency—the private sector can replace or complement government agencies in the delivery of culturally acceptable health services.

There continues to be legitimate discussion about the health conditions of immigrants. Several authors in this volume (Rasmussen, De Muynck, and Gailly and Ben Driss) suggest that immigrants in the European Union have worse health conditions and use health services and take sick leave more frequently than natives. On the other hand, Pierre Buekens and his collaborators review available data from Belgium and other European countries on birth outcomes of immigrants from North Africa. Their findings indicate that Belgian, French, and Dutch women have more low-weight deliveries than do North Africans (Algerians, Moroccans, and Tunisians) and that the frequency of preterm single deliveries is lower among North Africans than among Belgians. These findings mirror results of research in the United States among foreign-born women, Hispanics, and Asians. Evidence on both sides of the Atlantic suggests that as immigrants acculturate their health status deteriorates (Scribner 1996). If this perception is correct, pressures placed on immigrants to assimilate by policy makers and the larger society could have disastrous consequences for the health conditions of immigrants. From a public-health perspective, one could conclude that the receiving society should search for mechanisms to encourage immigrants to maintain their culture. The challenge to a modern society is to discover the mechanisms that allow diverse cultures to live together in harmony. Unfortunately, in the United States and in the European Union, the current political orientation is the opposite.

A culturally diverse society would support the idea that immigrants have their own autochthonous health services and be free to select between them and those available to the rest of the population. Until this utopian stage is achieved some countries are promoting through their public health services special provisions that facilitate immigrants' access to services. Health experts know that physical access to health services does not translate into utilization because some governments raise barriers and others fail to remove existing ones.

Some barriers are visible and others are less so. Several articles in the volume document existing obstacles to health service utilization and their impact on the quality of care. The contribution by Aimé De Muynck and the one by Hans Verrept and Fred Louckx provide an insightful view of the successes and limitations of special provisions in Belgium. De Muynck has documented for a number of years through his research that Belgian health services are not adapted to provide health care to Moroccan and Turkish patients, even if Moroccan and Turkish residents in Belgium are theoretically entitled, like natives, to have access to the national health services. In this study, findings from a survey of health-delivery institutions and of general practitioners allow De Muynck to conclude that as special provisions are currently used in Belgium, their impact on access and on quality is limited.

Verrept and Louckx examine the role of health advocates among

Turkish and Moroccan patients from interviews of health professionals and health advocates themselves. Health advocates are cultural brokers who besides acting as interpreters also brief health providers about cultural factors that may influence health conditions, explain to patients some dimensions of biomedical "culture" and the functioning of the health system, and advocate on behalf of ethnic patients. According to the authors, several factors reduce the effectiveness of this potentially useful resource. In addition to the complexity of cross-cultural communication in a health setting, advocates lack the training and skills necessary to interact effectively with health professionals. Several solutions are advanced to improve the outcome of the work done by advocates, including joint sessions between health professionals and advocates and a more formal recognition by health institutions and providers of the importance of advocates.

In recent years, Spain has been classified as a new immigration country within the European Union. A review of the literature and a survey of Moroccan construction workers in Madrid provide the information Antonio Ugalde used to study the health conditions of immigrant workers in Spain and their utilization of health services. In Spain there is evidence that the health conditions of immigrants deteriorate as a result of the social problems they face, such as substandard housing and sanitation conditions, pressures to send money home to their families, poor nutritional status, and, among undocumented workers, the fear of being apprehended. As in other countries of the Union, Spanish health services are not prepared to offer culturally different services to immigrants from North and Sub-Saharan Africa. Additionally, the law discriminates against foreign immigrants. Native indigent patients who cannot afford to pay the Social Security premium have free access to all health services, but the same right is denied to indigent legal immigrants.

In Spain the number of female labor immigrants is increasing. In the past most immigrant women were spouses who accompanied their husbands. This is not the case anymore, and an increasing number of women are migrating on their own. Consuelo Prado Martínez and her collaborators explore reproductive behavior variations of immigrant women in Madrid in relation to their region of origin. Their research examines the socioeconomic conditions before and after migration, health behavior, and clinical histories of respondents with emphasis on gynecological aspects. They found significant differences among migrant groups regarding depression, breast pain, skin alterations, headaches, edemas, backaches, and kidney aches. Variations in the frequency of gynecological checkups and in the use of birth control are also evident.

The two chapters on Spain suggest that immigration and living conditions in the receiving society produce anxiety, depression, and other mental health disorders. Antoine Gailly, a psychologist-anthropologist, and Redouane Ben Driss, a clinical psychologist, review the epidemiological aspects of immigrants' mental health and confirm that the stressors to which immigrants are exposed in receiving societies have negative mental health consequences. From their vantage point as clinicians at the Centruum voor Welzijnszorg in Brussels, the authors examine the many difficulties encountered in cross-cultural therapy and arrive at the disquieting conclusion that assistance to immigrants "does not respond to their needs anymore." According to the authors, there is an urgent need to rethink the therapeutic approach and to avoid the paternalism followed by therapists that tends to reinforce natives' negative perceptions of immigrants from developing countries.

We are aware that on both sides of the Atlantic public opinion has turned against immigrants. Hysteria is the term used by Marcelo M. Suárez-Orozco to describe current anti-immigrant feelings. In his essay he argues that natives' portrayal of immigrants as undesirable "parasites and criminals taking our limited and diminishing resources . . . is largely a projective mechanism serving primitive psychological functions in times of social malaise (p. 140)." It also serves, Suárez-Orozco adds, to trigger negative reactions from second-generation immigrants against autochthonous populations—to which, in a vicious circle of fear and hatred, the natives react. The constructed image of immigrants contrasts sharply with the reality described by researchers. In his own work with immigrant children, Suárez-Orozco found that achievement, hard work, and interdependence were more valued by Mexican than by Anglo students, a view supported by other studies. Suárez-Orozco's analysis of school performance leads to the revealing conclusion that the longer children are in school the more they become like American students, and lose their motivation to do well and to be respectful. In the case of education as in the case of health, assimilation has undesirable consequences.

Ximena Urrutia-Rojas and Néstor Rodríguez studied the migration of children who traveled on their own or in the company of other children from Central America to the United States. In their article in this volume, after presenting the sociodemographic characteristics, the authors look at the multiple traumatic experiences suffered by the children prior to migrating, during the migration, and upon arrival. More than 10 percent of the children assessed for anxiety disorders scored at or above the post-traumatic stress disorder (PTSD) cutoff score. That many of the children arriving from Central America are in need of professional psychological help is obvious. Unfortunately, the anti-immigration sentiment in the United States is not going to facilitate the provision of these vitally needed services. In the long run, the failure to assist them is bound to create additional problems for the children and for the receiving society.

This collection of papers corroborates our initial hypothesis that the issues and problems of immigration in the United States and the European Union have many commonalities and that much can be learned from examining the experiences, successes, and failures of both regions. As several chapters in this volume show, a number of pilot projects and studies are being conducted in the United States and the European Union to increase coverage, decrease exclusion, and make services more culturally appropriate to users, but frequently these efforts are carried out in isolation. Collaborative research among scholars of members states of the European Union and of the United States could be useful in sharing innovations, in avoiding the same errors, and in strengthening proposals presented to policy makers.

ACKNOWLEDGMENTS

In addition to the support given by the Andalusian School of Public Health and the International Migration and Human Rights Project, the European Commission and the Inter-University Program for Latino Research provided financial assistance without which the meeting could not have taken place. The Euro-Arab University also helped us at the early stage of planning with sound advice and logistics.

We should give special thanks to several people at the Andalusian School of Public Health: Dr. Catalá Villanueva, director; Dr. Manuel Keenoy, academic director; and Dr. López Fernández, research coordinator. Prof. Olga Solas handled the many time-consuming details that a host institution must resolve for this type of event, including the search for funding, provision of simultaneous translation, and invitations to Spanish and Maghrebian scholars. The link between the University of Texas and the Andalusian School of Public Health would not have been possible without the personal commitment and understanding of Dr. Oleaga Usategui, who is the school's studies coordinator. Margarita López Buitrago, the school's secretarial services coordinator, took a personal interest in ensuring that the workshop participants had a memorable and comfortable stay in Granada.

Thanks are due in Austin as well. The dean of liberals arts at the

University of Texas, Dr. Sheldon Ekland-Olson, is a colleague, friend, and visionary administrator who truly understands the importance of international studies in our global society. From the moment we approached him with the idea of the workshop, he never hesitated to assist and encourage us. Raquel Márquez, a graduate sociology student at UT, filled multiple roles during the preparation of the workshop: research assistant, accountant, travel agent, and troubleshooter for all the problems that commonly arise in the organization of international meetings.

Finally, we need to extend our appreciation to the Center for Mexican American Studies, the Center for Middle Eastern Studies, and the College of Liberal Arts of the University of Texas and the Inter-University Program for Latino Research for providing funding and support in the preparation and publication of this volume. Thanks also to Víctor Guerra, coordinator of publications at the Center for Mexican American Studies, who guided the process from beginning to end, and Teri Sperry, who meticulously edited the manuscript.

Reference

Scribner, E. 1996. "Editorial: Paradox as Paradigm—The Health Outcomes of Mexican Americans." *American Journal of Public Health* 86: 303–304.

Health and Social Services among
International Labor Migrants

1

International Migration and Health in the European Union

Lars Rasmussen

Official statistics show that in 1992 the net migration of the fifteen member countries of the European Union (EUR-15) was 1.2 million persons. In 1984 net migration was close to zero. It began to turn positive in 1985, increasing rapidly from 1988 onward and surpassing the two million figure in 1990. On the other hand, in 1995 there were between eight and ten million permanent immigrants living legally or illegally in EUR-15. This figure gives an idea of the magnitude of the health problems faced by the Union. Statistics indicate that the majority of migrants are males and on the average younger than the rest of the population. It is expected, though, that migration will not have any impact on the size and age distribution of the population of the member states of the European Union until 2025; by then net migration should begin to fall again. By the early part of the twenty-first century, because of falling birth rates in the member states of EUR-15 and the aging of the population, the labor force may be insufficient to maintain a healthy economy and generate a surplus to cover the needs of the elderly European population. If the projections are correct, migration from outside of the Union might be necessary to alleviate the problem. Of course, much of the needed migration will come from developing countries.

We could look at migration from a different perspective. About one million persons per year, the majority of whom come from developing countries, move permanently to the traditional receivers of migrants: the United States, Canada, and Australia. It is also interesting to note that as many as seventy million temporary migrants are working legally and illegally in these and other countries. If we include international travelers, tourists, and long-term migrant workers, the total number of migrants will approximate about one billion persons by the end of the century. Refugees constitute an important component of the international migration flow. In 1992 the official estimate of internationally displaced refugees in the world was about fifteen million, the majority of whom are from developing nations in Asia, Africa, Latin America, and Eastern Europe.

Migration is not a new phenomenon; historically it is more the rule than the exception. At various times in the history of Europe, whole peoples moved across the continent. The traces of these migrations can be found in the way ethnic groups and languages are spread on the European map. The reasons for migration have not changed either; they include political upheavals and unrest, natural calamities, economic insecurity and famine, and religious and political persecution. Only the impact of the migratory movements has changed, probably because of economic and social development. It can also be suggested that our capacity to cope with migration is today considerably better than it has ever been in the past, but often the appropriate action is not taken because it may be politically unpopular.

It is an irrefutable fact that historically rapid economic growth and development have gone hand in hand with migration. For example, the cheap labor that the United States received from Europe at the turn of the century greatly facilitated the country's economic development. After World War II, West Germany owed its rapid reconstruction to the influx of refugees from East Germany and later to unskilled labor from Turkey. Austria has likewise profited from the arrival of approximately 900,000 temporary workers, and France has also benefited from millions of *"pied noirs"* (a term frequently used to identify migrants from Sub-Saharan Africa) and immigrants from the Maghreb.

In the nation-state at a regional level and in the European Union at a national level, the mobility of labor or migration increases with variations in the economic cycle. In economic theory, labor, capital, and technologies are factors of production. Factors of production are movable: we have seen, for example, large amounts of capital moving to Southeast Asia, where labor is cheap, and for the same reason technologies have been transferred to China. Thus, transfers of capital and technology are means of preventing the migration of persons. One of the goals of the Treaty of Rome signed in 1957 is the free movement of persons, capital, goods, and services. Consequently, migration within the Union is an important element of EUR-15, and the protection of migrants within the Union has become an important component of its social policy.

If we look at migration from a health perspective, we cannot ignore that in EUR-15 the physical health of immigrants is poorer than the health of native populations (see De Muynck in this volume). Such a reality has or should have an impact on health care expenditures and the organization of health services. Tuberculosis is increasingly more resistant to drug treatment, and prevalence rates among migrants is on the rise. Immigrants also suffer higher rates of accidents, and problems related to long-term care, isolation, and poor nutrition among the older people in the "extended families" that do not have the economic resources to help them. Studies have shown that migrants have a higher incidence of psychiatric disorders (see Gailly and Ben Driss in this volume). Stress and anxiety caused by slow processing of applications for asylum and by ineffective social integration and economic incorporation explain in part the higher rates (see Ugalde in this volume).

Social and noncommunicable lifestyle hazards also threaten immigrants in the European Union. The receiving countries have always thought that immigrants from Eastern European countries and the developing nations pose a health problem to the native populations because of the risk of communicable diseases such as tuberculosis and imported tropical diseases. But perhaps immigrants should be warned that they are the ones who run the risk of being infected by tuberculosis and other diseases because of poor housing, malnutrition, weakened immune systems, and poverty in general. At the same time, immigrants are also exposed to a range of new lifestyle diseases such as asthma, heart disease, stroke, and certain types of cancer.

The health systems of the member states of EUR-15 are not adapted to the health needs of immigrants (see De Muynck, and Verrept and Louckx in this volume). The systems are fundamentally monocultural and thus poorly equipped to meet the needs of societies that are increasingly diverse in their linguistic and cultural compositions. There is a pressing need to organize health services and special provisions for different groups and subcultures. The absence of multicultural health services implies that members of nonnative ethnic groups very often experience difficulties in their interaction with and utilization of health and social services designed for a different population. Health policy makers, administrators, and providers need to take into account the cultural universes of migrants.

Immigrants in EUR-15 generally have higher rates of sick leave and a higher use of social benefits. These are not services of choice, but rather are caused by inadequate host structures and circumstances beyond their control. But how to explain it to the host society in times of economic recession when the European governments are trying to reduce the health budgets and reorganize pension systems in order to qualify for membership in the European Monetary Union?

If migration were regarded as only temporary by both the migrants and the host countries, perhaps many of the social and economic conflicts, which arise where there is pressure on either side to see migration as a permanent move, would be reduced. The progress of nationalist movements in recent elections all over Europe shows that the European Union has perhaps reached the limit of its capacity to absorb and integrate migrants and refugees. Even Sweden, which has always been very liberal, has recently introduced a much more restrictive immigration policy. Now obtaining the status of political refugee in Sweden has become more difficult, and economic refugees are turned back. It has also become more difficult to obtain a Swedish work permit. The same is occurring in Germany. This is part of the policy of adopting common and compatible rules in order to later make the free movement of persons including migrants and refugees possible.

Given these conditions in EUR-15, it would have been expected that the European Commission would have undertaken some action in the health sector. However, the Treaty of Rome did not give the commission specific powers in this sector. In the early days of the European Community, there was no global health strategy or policy, with the exception of specific actions concerning health and safety at work and policies on socioeconomic and environmental issues that also had public health consequences.

Only with the Treaty on European Union, also known as the Treaty of Maastricht (1992), did the commission finally obtain shared powers with member states in the field of health. It occurred not so much because of concern with the health of European citizens as because of a desire to cut down soaring costs for health care due to the economic recession. The new powers were anchored in Article 3(0) and Article 129(a) of the treaty. It is the responsibility of the Union to assure a high level of health in the member states, but it is symptomatic that the competence of the commission is limited basically to health promotion and prevention, or information, education, and training. Some member states even feel that the commission has too many powers and that health should be removed from the treaty altogether. However, at the time of this writing health is not on the agenda of the 1996 Inter-Governmental Conference (IGC).

Dr. Horst Seehofer, Minister of Health of the German Federal Republic, said before the Committee for Health and Environment of the European Parliament in December 1995 that the time had come to create a real health policy for EUR-15, but one that would be subject to the principle of subsidiarity, a principle which needs first to be defined. In practice this means that public health is more or less the exclusive responsibility of each member state. Union interference can be tolerated only in certain areas and under certain circumstances.

The European Union has not and still does not have an integrated approach to the health needs of immigrants. Health responsibilities are scattered all over the commission's general directorates, and health dimensions are discovered in all Union policies. The commission will participate in international conferences and timidly state its position, as it did in 1990 at the First International Conference on Migration Medicine and again in 1992 at the Second International Conference on Migration and Health. But there is little or no action or attempt to put together a coherent strategy, for three reasons. First, there are no funds or staff available for such action. Second, migrants have no strong pressure groups or lobbyists to plead their cause. Third, it would imply interference in national affairs. On average, member states spend 8.1 percent of their GNPs on health care, and they are very conscious of European Community interference in such an important area. Where large amounts of money are involved, integration slows down.

Since migrants from developing nations are marginalized in host societies, health interventions undertaken specifically for native marginal populations are frequently applicable to them. This is the case, for example, in disease-specific programs such as tuberculosis and, in general, health promotion interventions. In the case of AIDS we find information campaigns in member states that are specifically targeted to immigrants from developing nations.

The General Directorate for Social Affairs has a unit working exclusively on migration. It supports projects in the health field such as psychiatric assistance for immigrant children, implementation of training programs for physicians and nurses based on the cultural and religious needs of patients of ethnic minority origin, publication of thematic guides for medical staff working with immigrants, and information campaigns in Italy against circumcision of African women. The latter project is a good example of how to design an effective prevention campaign while taking into account differences in cultural perception.

The most important activity of the General Directorate for Social Affairs is the work it does in helping immigrants to integrate into local and national societies. It is the understanding of the directorate that by doing so it may prevent a large number of mental disorders and traumas among immigrants and thereby decrease social tensions between the host countries and the immigrants. The European Commission proposed that 1997 should be a European year against racism. It was a bold decision, considering the anti-immigration positions of many people in the Union, but it is in line with the 1989 Community Charter of the Fundamental Social Rights of Workers, which underlined the importance of combating every form of discrimination based on sex, color, race, opinion, and belief. At the time of this writing, the United Kingdom has blocked this proposal in the Social Council as part of its strategy to paralyze the European Union until there is a lift of the export ban on British beef products imposed because of the health risk of the spread of Bovine Spongiform Encephalopathy (BSE) to humans.

The commission should take the initiative within the existing policies and help member states to resolve immigrants' health problems. For example, there are not enough exchanges of information between countries about health services and programs for migrants. From an economic point of view, such an approach would be sound. The commission also has the possibility, through the Social and Regional Funds with the tacit consent of member states, to build hospitals and set up medical services specifically targeted to multicultural users and to educate and train medical staff to function in multicultural and multilingual environments. So far no member state has taken advantage of this opportunity.

The free movement of goods and services, capital, and persons is one of the three main pillars of the European Union, but until the present time foreign residents from outside of the Union living in one of the member states cannot legally move and work in other member states.[1] The Union is currently discussing ways to change this situation by approving legislation on access to its territory and on the free movement of any person legally resident in any member state. It is important when individuals move from one country to another within the European Union that they continue to enjoy basic social protections. The commission has always supported the view that this principle should be applicable to all persons who are legal residents, including migrants. When approved the new legislation will have significant spillover effects in the social and health spheres to the extent that legal third-country immigrants will enjoy the same protection as nationals.

The provisions of Title VI of the Treaty of Rome cover both the movement of non-Community nationals into and out of the member states by crossing external borders and the situation of non-Community nationals admitted to member states. At the same time, the third-country nationals who have legal residency in member states are protected by Community law regarding issues such as labor, equal treatment for men and women, health and safety, and education and training, and they can be beneficiaries of Structural Funds.[2]

The Treaty on the European Economic Area and association agreements with countries such as Tunisia (treaty signed July 17, 1995) and Morocco (treaty signed February 26, 1996) would open—when implemented—the borders of the European Union for people from these countries who would like to come and work in the Union. These temporary migrant workers would enjoy the same rights to social and health benefits as any Union citizen. At the same time, in an attempt to reduce outmigration pressures in the sending nations, the association agreements with Morocco and Tunisia indicate that the Union will support development programs in these countries.

The principle of nondiscrimination would apply to legal migrant workers with a valid work permit from these countries, and they would enjoy the same rights as national workers regarding wages and social security. Yet they would not be able to move freely within the Union, a situation that may be in contradiction with the principle of free movement of labor embraced by the Treaty of Rome. In all these matters the national legislation of member states applies and would determine if these migrants may bring spouses or children, but in general they would not be permitted to do so because working permits have a time limitation. Member states consider that bringing the family promotes permanent residency with the intention of eventually acquiring nationality, an idea that goes against the concept of a temporary work permit.

One of the basic objectives of the European Commission's social programs for migrants is to aid in their social integration within the territory of a member state and in the incorporation into the labor market of those who can be gainfully employed. Another basic objective is to produce social cohesion, which is important for the health and survival of a society and applies to both natives and immigrants. Sweden has been very successful in this respect.

The 1992 Council Recommendation for the convergence of social protection objectives and policies sets out a clear definition of policy objectives in the health area: (1) to maintain and develop a high-quality health care system geared to the evolving needs of the population, the treatment of pathologies, the development of therapies, and prevention, and (2) to ensure that all legal residents have access to necessary health care as well as preventive services.

The present trend in the European Union is to limit immigration in order to provide employment for nationals and protect social gains. To this end, Luxembourg, for example, has an exception clause that restricts the free movement of persons from the Union and allows the government to put a stop to sudden mass migration. But the aging of the population in the Union may force member states to change their views on immigration. If the demographic projections are true—in other words, if the ratio of the population above 65 years to the active population increases drastically and is not compensated by productivity increases—Europe may once again need to import labor in order to protect social achievements, retirement age, and other benefits of the welfare state.

The European Union countries are actively limiting the inflow of labor from third countries. And in order to facilitate the free movement of all legal residents in the territory of the Union, the member states will have to harmonize immigration and refugee policies. Padraiag Flynn, commissioner for social affairs, has said repeatedly that the ultimate goal of social and health policy in the European Union is that any person legally resident in the Union should enjoy the same rights as do nationals in regard to seeking employment wherever they want and to social protection, including access to health care, in accordance with Articles 3(0) and 129(a) of the Treaty on European Union.

Notes

The author is presently principal administrator at the Public Health Directorate of the European Commission. This essay does not necessarily reflect the views of the Commission of the European Communities and is in no way an indication of the commission's future position in this area.

1. The other two pillars are collaboration in the field of justice, policing, and related activities, and defense (external policy).

2. The Structural Funds include the European Regional Development Fund (ERDF), the European Social Fund (ESF), and the European Agricultural Guarantee and Development Fund (EAGDF). The purpose of these funds is to reinforce the efforts made by the national governments, the regional authorities, and private investors. In the 1994–99 period these funds amount to 141 billion ECU (one U.S. dollar = 0.788 ECU)—one third of the entire European Union budget. The funds are meant to enhance the economic and social cohesion of the European Union by supporting developing areas through the restructuring of industrial regions, providing aid to reduce long-term unemployment, creating jobs for young people, modernizing agriculture, and helping less-developed agricultural regions (such as those where mountain farming is practiced).

2

Meeting the Social Service Needs of Mexican Immigrants in the United States

Yolanda C. Padilla

The comparative study of the social and health policies formulated by receiving countries to meet the basic needs of immigrants is of special significance in various parts of the world today. However, this issue has received little attention in the United States, particularly in terms of social service provision. The objective of this paper is to assess the response of the social service system in the United States in meeting the needs of immigrants, particularly Mexican immigrants living along the U.S.–Mexico border, and to consider the need for international collaboration in social service delivery to this population. The paper is divided into three parts, examining (1) the approach to international social work with immigrants in the United States, including the political and economic barriers to international collaboration between the United States and Mexico in human service provision to immigrants; (2) current U.S. policies related to the delivery of social services to immigrants; and (3) critical issues in serving immigrants from the perspective of social work practitioners, based on a case study of the U.S. border region near Mexico, an area with a disproportionately high concentration of Mexican immigrants.

The poverty conditions of both cities and rural areas in developing nations represent some of the most compelling problems of our time. Such conditions have motivated many to immigrate to more prosperous neighboring nations in hope of a better future. Nowhere in the world are the differences in wealth between bordering countries as vast as they are between the United States and Mexico. And nowhere else in the world is the movement of people across international boundaries as prevalent as it is between these two countries. It is estimated that nearly 250 million people cross the border annually between the United States and Mexico, making it the most frequently crossed border in the world (Suárez y Toriello and Chávez Alzaga 1996). Certainly these population movements have important ramifications for adjoining countries, particularly for so-cial service delivery, because families are connected across international boundaries.

The movement of people from Mexico to the United States takes on a variety of forms, including permanent immigration, temporary labor migration, and commuting. Between 1981 and 1991 people originating from Latin America and the Caribbean made up the largest flow of per-manent immigrants to the United States. Forty-seven percent of immi-grants in the United States during this period originated from Latin America and the Caribbean, primarily Mexico (Rolph 1992). In addition, the most recent figures from the U.S. Bureau of the Census show that the rate of Mexican immigration has increased steadily since the pre-1960s period. In 1980 a full 33 percent of all permanent Mexican immi-grants in the United States had arrived within the previous five years (Rolph 1992).

Mexican immigration to the United States is directly related to the internal movement of people from the interior of Mexico to the border region. In order to escape poverty, many people from rural areas in the interior historically have migrated to the border. It is estimated that in 1974, 25 percent of the population of Mexico's borderland cities was made up of migrants (Lorey 1993). In the 1970s, 1980s, and 1990s, they have increasingly migrated to U.S. cities in search of work (Lorey 1993, Martínez 1992). A second important migration flow from Mexico into the United States is made up of temporary labor migrants. For example, approximately 60 to 70 percent of migrant farmworkers in the state of New Mexico travel from Mexico to the United States to work in agricul-ture on a temporary basis (Skolnick 1995b). Finally, significant numbers of Mexican commuters cross the U.S. border daily to work, to obtain medical services, for recreation, and to shop (Lorey 1993).

The Approach to International Social Work with Immigrants in the United States

A review of the literature reveals that in the United States the concern with social service delivery to immigrants (including legal immigrants, refugees, asylees, and undocumented immigrants) has been largely lim-ited to a concern with providing culturally sensitive services (Christensen 1992, Drachman 1992, Le-Doux and Stephens 1992). In fact, a recent book titled *Social Work with Immigrants and Refugees* (Ryan 1992) points out that "in the host countries there is often a lot of talk about the subject of immigration, but nothing much is being done about it. The scarcity of related literature in major social work periodicals reflects this" (pp. xii–xiv). Yet social work with immigrants requires a broader perspective on the social work role, specifically a more international approach. Defined in its broadest sense, international social work—including social work with immigrants—implies international cooperation among social work professionals to work on social problems that transcend national borders (Estes 1992, Healy 1995).

The literature suggests that international issues in service delivery to immigrants should include knowledge of immigration dynamics, a comparative view of international social welfare policies, an understanding of how the social and economic context of the host country restricts the effectiveness of practice methods, and an awareness of immigrants' cultural background (Ahearn and Athey 1991, Estes 1992, Hokenstad, Khinduka, and Midgley 1992). Sherraden and Martin (1994: 369) conceptualize effective social work with immigrants from an international perspective based on an understanding of the context of their former lives and the circumstances surrounding their immigration. Specifically, they suggest that social workers take into account (1) differences in the nature of informal networks of assistance and formal social welfare services in countries of origin and the United States and (2) the immigration process, including the factors influencing the decision to migrate, settlement patterns, the role of social support networks, and the political and economic links to the communities of origin. In addition, social workers need to acknowledge the differences in knowledge, attitudes, and practices of people from different countries. Therefore, a truly multicultural approach is a minimum requirement for successful and effective intervention with immigrant populations in receiving countries.

Moreover, in terms of direct service delivery to immigrant families, Leiper de Monchy (1991) suggests specific program components that help eliminate some of the Western bias that may exist among professionals in the United States. The first recommendation is that agencies employ bilingual and bicultural staff who are familiar with the immigrants' traditions and values. Furthermore, staff need to be sensitive to the fact that immigrants may be quite unfamiliar with how the U.S. system works and thus may need information about access and service procedures. Second, in cases when immigrants may be escaping from political violence in their countries of origin, service providers must be knowledgeable of the past traumatic experiences and the effects of those experiences on their psychological, emotional, and physical well-being. Third, in order to establish trust, agencies should reach out and establish linkages with the migrant community. Finally, service providers should integrate the methods of healing that are traditionally part of the immigrants' lives. In sum, social workers recognize that (1) social services in the receiving country are needed to help in the successful integration of immigrants, and should be responsive to the unique needs of diverse immigrant groups, and (2) an understanding of the conditions in the country of origin is important in providing adequate assistance because the conditions faced in the sending community influence social background and the reasons for moving and, thus, the social integration of immigrants (Sherraden and Martin 1994).

Although Americans do talk about social service delivery in terms of the problems immigrants face in the United States, human services policy formulation is almost completely disconnected from the immigrants' countries of origin. Clearly, service providers view conditions in the country of origin principally as part of a "pre-migration stage," that is, the social, political, and economic factors that impacted the decision to migrate at the time of departure (Drachman 1992, Jacob 1994). However, once the immigrant moves to the "transit" and "resettlement" stages, factors associated with the country of origin are not considered as relevant, nor are they seen as having an impact on the receiving country (other than by influencing the rate of immigration). As a result, intervention modalities with immigrants are limited in scope. For example, Drachman and Halberstadt (1992) suggest that a potential role for international social work would be to conduct educational programs provided by the United States in sending countries. Potential immigrants would be provided with information about the difficulties they are likely to encounter in the United States related to housing, employment, high resettlement expenses, lowered status, and so on. The idea would be "to dispel myths about life in the United States and reduce unrealistic expectations held by many émigrés" (Drachman and Halberstadt 1992: 76).

Such a nationally focused approach to international social work in the United States is to be expected given that our immigrants—Asians, Africans, Europeans, Central and South Americans—come from far-off lands. However, the case of Mexican immigrants on the U.S. side of the U.S.–Mexico border region is different, and the impact of this sending community on the area is substantial. Here we cannot speak of immigrants as individuals disconnected from their country of origin. In this community, the movement across the international boundary involves more than the movement of people, but also a level of interdependence due to common economic, health, and social problems on both sides of the border (Lorey 1993). For example, the problem of street children in certain cities in Mexico, such as Juárez, Chihuahua, is increasingly shared by the neighboring U.S. city of El Paso, Texas (Peralta 1992). As a result of the symbiotic relationship between the contiguous border areas of the United States and Mexico, meeting the social service needs of immigrants requires that the two countries work together. Thus, even within the current restrictive policy of the United States toward immigration described below, it is still necessary to address the very real problems faced by the border immigrant community.

In fields such as urban planning (Herzog 1985), the environment (Schepps 1994), and health (Asociación Fronteriza Mexicano-Estadounidense de Salud 1990), the need for cooperative planning models has been more clearly articulated than it has been in social work. According to Herzog (1985: 31), an expert in urban planning, "while interdependence between settlements along the [U.S.–Mexico] border grows stronger, politics and decision-making remain two separate, and indeed disparate, national jurisdictions." This results in potential mismanagement of problems due to divergent goals, policies, and planning strategies. Therefore, a proposed revised agenda given the "spillover" effect of problems in both directions across international boundaries includes (1) developing plans that address the concerns of each country but blend the needs on both sides of the border and (2) coordinating services in a way that is beneficial to both sides (Herzog 1985).

In the social services, joint work among U.S. and Mexican professionals in the planning and delivery of health and social services along the U.S.–Mexico border might include binational agreements for carrying out social welfare programs. For example, such collaboration could occur via joint research, social policy analysis, planning, program development, advocacy, public education, and coordination (Kelley, Balderrabano, and Briseño 1986). There is a growing need for social service providers to work on intercountry cases related to adoption, custody, divorce, and human rights (Healy 1995). In addition to coordination of cases between social service agencies, cooperative arrangements could be made between other public organizations, such as schools (for example, involving the exchange of student health records and following up on students with special needs who transfer to schools across the border).

Even with the understanding that effective services for Mexican immigrants require international collaboration, little attention has been given to social service delivery issues affecting immigrants on the border. The concerns on this particular U.S. border are further complicated by the fact that, unlike Canada, the only other nation with which the United States shares a border, Mexico is a developing country. Nevertheless, neither the United States nor Mexico has a comprehensive policy on this matter.

Political and Economic Barriers to International Collaboration

Part of the explanation for the limited level of international social work with immigrants and the lack of collaboration between the United States and Mexico in the delivery of social services to Mexican immigrants is associated with political, social, and economic barriers. No single structure exists to facilitate international collaboration between the countries that form North America (aside from the newly created North American Free Trade Agreement [NAFTA], which is solely a commercial agreement). Indeed, although policies related to immigration from developing countries and international collaboration are being formulated and actively promoted by the social work community in Europe (Fernández Franco 1992), no such dialogue is taking place in the United States. The lack of such a policy-making mechanism weakens attempts by local governments to set up international projects because they lack the support of national governments, as comparative analyses of North America and Europe show (Hansen 1983, Herzog 1985).

Furthermore, in addition to the vast inequalities in power and resources between the two countries, there are important differences between the two in terms of their social welfare systems, the perspectives of social service professionals, and social work roles and practice methods (Aguilar in press; Kelley, Balderrabano, and Briseño 1986; Midgley 1990, 1992; Durán, Licea, and Duraza 1994). First, in contrast to the decentralized system of social welfare in the United States, Mexico's social welfare planning is centralized in the federal government. In the United States many health and social welfare services are implemented by state and local governments. However, when it comes to sources of funding in the United States, many basic needs are met through federal and state public assistance programs. In Mexico, although the social welfare system is centralized, the means for providing basic services is more commonly through local community participation, due to the limited availability of federal government funds. Second, professionals in Mexico, as in other developing countries, tend to approach social problems from a macro perspective and rely heavily on local community resources and informal support networks. This is in contrast to the more agency-based micro-level methods of U.S. human service professionals that focus on individual and family interventions. Third, social work roles and community practice methods vary in the two countries, reflecting their stage of global development. In Mexico, the role of a community practitioner is to raise political consciousness and to form self-sufficient organizations. On the other hand, community practice in the United States tends to focus on social planning and policy analysis activities.

The basic differences in the social service delivery systems between the United States and Mexico reflect political, economic, and cross-cultural factors. Although the existence of these variations certainly poses problems for international collaboration, a mutual understanding of the dynamics of each country can facilitate efforts at bilateral cooperation.

Current U.S. Policy on Social Service Provision to Immigrants

Given the powerful political and economic barriers to international collaboration, the current U.S. policy related to the delivery of social services to immigrants is quite narrowly defined and does not include provisions for international agreements. Although services for immigrants are in fact provided from a variety of sources through nonprofit and church-based organizations, U.S. federal policy regarding entitlements and other public benefits for new immigrants is weak and inconsistent. Currently, specific policies for most social welfare provisions to immigrants are limited to legal immigrants and refugees. Federal government services have been provided to immigrants and refugees within the framework of two programs: the Refugee Resettlement Program and the Immigration Reform and Control Act provision for State Legalization Impact Assistance Grants (SLIAG). A third and influential policy development is Proposition 187, a State of California initiative, passed in 1994, that focuses on the denial of a wide range of public and social services to immigrants. New federal welfare reform legislation passed in 1996 reflects the influence of Proposition 187. Finally, state and local policies play a major role in supporting human service provision to immigrants.

REFUGEE RESETTLEMENT PROGRAM

Created under the Refugee Act of 1980, this immigration policy guarantees access to social support, including transportation, relocation allowances, job training, and public assistance programs, such as Aid to Families with

Dependent Children, Supplementary Security Income, and Medicaid (Rolph 1992). This assistance is restricted to refugees, people who gained entry into the United States based on a petition for entry which they originated from their own home country on the grounds of fear of persecution in their country. However, asylees, people who have received asylum based on the same grounds but who have requested and are granted residency in the United States once they have actually entered the country, are not eligible for social service benefits (unless they obtain permanent status). The Refugee Resettlement Program is administered by the Office of Refugee Resettlement, Family Support Administration of the U.S. Department of Health and Human Services. The program provides funding to the states, which then contract with local entities to provide resettlement services for refugees. Funding is allocated to provide employment-related services and to help localities that are heavily impacted by refugee populations, including grants to states to fund self-help indigenous organizations (Le-Doux and Stephens 1992).

STATE LEGALIZATION IMPACT ASSISTANCE GRANTS

The State Legalization Impact Assistance Grants under the Immigration Reform and Control Act of 1986 were created as a mechanism to help states and local governments provide public health, public assistance, social services, and education exclusively to previously undocumented immigrants who under this act were granted legal status in the United States (Le-Doux and Stephens 1992, Rolph 1992). It is important to note, however, that legalized persons were restricted from receiving specific social services in general based on the Immigration and Naturalization Service's "public charge" criteria for application for citizenship status (Plascencia and Wong 1991). Over three million people applied for legalization under this one-time program, which ended in 1994. However, based on a study conducted in Texas in 1991, only a small proportion of newly legalized persons reported receiving any assistance from government programs (Plascencia and Wong 1991).

PROPOSITION 187 AND THE WELFARE REFORM ACT OF 1996

One of the most important policy developments related to the provision of social services to immigrants was a proposition passed on November 18, 1994, in the state of California. Proposition 187 (1994) denies public social services to undocumented persons and furthermore requires that social service providers report persons illegally seeking services. Specifically, it places limits on all health services (except hospital emergency treatment) to noncitizens and legal immigrants. It also denies public education and postsecondary college training to immigrants who are not living in the United States legally. The push behind Proposition 187 to deny services to undocumented immigrants (i.e., those who have entered the United States illegally), and in some cases to certain legal immigrants, is reflected in new federal immigration reform legislation. Under the 1996 Welfare Reform Act, for example, public assistance for legal immigrants will also be restricted. Most legal immigrants who are not yet citizens will be ineligible for old-age or disability payments under the Supplementary Security Income program and health coverage under the Medicaid program, food stamps, and other basic social services (Analysis of Federal Welfare Reform, August 14, 1996). School nutrition programs for children and prenatal care for pregnant women will also be denied. Proposition 187 in the state of California is currently under appeal because it is considered unconstitutional under U.S. law, but the federal legislation was signed into law on August 22, 1996. Such policies suggest that under current budget cuts, the provision of social services to immigrants is likely to receive low priority.

STATE AND LOCAL POLICIES

In light of the absence of a comprehensive federal policy on the provision of social services to immigrants, state and local governments have been forced to take a significant role. State and local governments deliver the majority of the services under current federal policy. Besides the programs implemented as a result of the federal policies described above, states have also provided bilingual education for children with limited English (under the Bilingual Education Act) and emergency and prenatal medical services to undocumented immigrants (under the Medicaid public assistance program) (Rosenberg 1991). Examples of several state initiatives illustrate the roles state and local governments have played in addition to implementing federally mandated programs. Such initiatives include the development of a campaign to provide basic orientation services to all immigrants in New York, the creation of a task force to examine the state policies and programs for new immigrants in Oregon (Rosenberg 1991), and coordination of services for immigrant children, youth, and families in the areas of mental health, child welfare, public health, and social services in Massachusetts (Leiper de Monchy 1991).

Furthermore, in spite of proposed immigration reform, currently immigrants and refugees often receive social services through channels serving the poor or from universal public services (Rolph 1992). Generally, such programs currently do not discriminate in the provision of social services between native and immigrant groups. For example, by law every child in the United States regardless of legal status is entitled to public education. Similarly, all children are entitled to child protective services in situations of child abuse or neglect. Other services, including subsidized housing, legal aid, and shelters for the homeless usually do not require proof of legal status in the United States. In terms of health services, some local communities who have such services simply require proof of residency in the local city or county. Currently, children of undocumented immigrants born in the United States hold full citizenship rights and are entitled to federal public assistance, such as food stamps, Medicaid, and Aid to Families with Dependent Children, and public health services, such as vaccinations, although the parents are not eligible for these services.

Nevertheless, the entitlement to these services by undocumented and certain legal immigrants and children of undocumented immigrants is currently being challenged in the United States as part of a strong anti-welfare and anti-immigration reform movement. The focus is shifting to strong controls on the entrance of foreigners, particularly illegal immigrants, into the United States. Indeed, the express purpose of the Immigration Reform and Control Act of 1986 was not to provide social services to immigrants but rather to control illegal immigration by providing amnesty to persons already residing in the United States illegally and by tightening sanctions on employers who hire undocumented persons (Fix and Passel 1994). By far the largest group of immigrants affected by this law were undocumented workers from Mexico, Central America, and the Caribbean: about two million received legal immigrant status (Rolph 1992).

Clearly, the policies guiding the provision of social services to immigrants in the United States currently are quite limited and fragmented and do not contribute to strategic planning. Moreover, there is little evidence based on formal evaluation to support the effectiveness of current programs in helping immigrants to adapt to life in the United States (Rosenberg 1991). All in all, the United States has an ambiguous policy on human service provision to facilitate the integration of immigrants and no policy on international collaboration with sending communities. A recent policy analysis of U.S. immigration conducted by the Program for Research on Immigration Policy (Rolph 1992: 58) concluded: "Migration has become a world phenomenon, and the search for policies to deal with the internal and external problems of immigration will require increasing dialogue and closer *international cooperation,* particularly among the western nations. National immigration policies, which have been viewed as internal matters, may increasingly be viewed as integral to national security and foreign policy" (emphasis added). The conditions of the region of the United States bordering Mexico described below suggest that a more comprehensive immigration policy is needed, one that incorporates efforts toward the social, political, and economic incorporation of immigrants.

Critical Issues in Serving Immigrants from the Perspective of Social Service Providers: A Case Study of the U.S.–Mexico Border Region

Although people from Mexico migrate to all parts of the United States, social service provision to Mexican immigrants is a critical problem in communities bordering Mexico, where Mexican immigrants tend to concentrate. An estimated 25 percent of the population of U.S. communities bordering Mexico is composed of immigrants (Lorey 1993). Fifty-five percent of the people who live in U.S. border communities are of Mexican origin (*U.S.–Mexico Border Health Statistics* 1990). The situation of the state of Texas, one of the four U.S. states bordering Mexico, illustrates the unique problems of meeting the basic social service needs of the Mexican immigrant border population in the United States. Texas faces some of the most critical problems in the border region. The U.S. Bureau of the Census found that in 1990, four of the five poorest cities in the country with populations of at least 100,000 were located on the Texas-Mexico border (Skolnick 1995a). Although formal research on social service provision to immigrants on the U.S.–Mexico border is almost nonexistent, the case study reported below provides a preliminary assessment of the problems facing these communities from the perspective of human service providers. The study was part of a larger policy research project focusing on the status of Hispanic children and families living in the U.S.–Mexico border region (*Hispanic Children in Texas* 1995).[1] It included a series of focused group interviews and over fifty individual interviews with providers in a number of social service areas, including child welfare, juvenile delinquency, public health, schools, teen pregnancy, mental health, and general social services. It was conducted by the School of Social Work at the University of Texas at Austin in conjunction with a public policy center, the Center for Public Policy Priorities.

THEORETICAL AND EMPIRICAL BACKGROUND

The purpose of the study was to gather information on the status of families in border communities from social service providers and to make it available to social policy makers at the local, state, and federal levels. It builds on a limited but growing body of literature on the contributions of social service providers to U.S. border social policy issues (Daigle 1994, Kelley, Balderrabano, and Briseño 1986). Social service providers are uniquely situated to understand the social problems in a community, to interpret them to citizens and officials, and to recommend policy alternatives. They directly provide services to people at all stages of life, and they have access and knowledge about environmental conditions and the adequacy of the response of social service systems to those who need support.

A demographic profile of the area provides the context for understanding the recommendations of the providers. On almost every measure (health, education, income), Mexican immigrants fare worse than the general U.S. population and worse than their native-born counterparts (Bean, Chapa, Berg, and Sowards 1994). For Mexican immigrants living in the U.S. region bordering Mexico, problems are compounded by the poor social and economic situation in their communities and further complicated because of the conditions of poverty in Mexico. The area of Texas that borders Mexico is made up of fourteen counties, stretching from El Paso County in the western end of Texas to Cameron County in the southeastern end. These counties contain a disproportionately large immigrant population. Nearly 25 percent of persons living in the Texas border area are classified as immigrants (foreign born), the vast majority of whom are Mexican, whereas the state average is 9 percent, according to the 1990 Census (U.S. Bureau of the Census 1993). And in high-density–poverty rural areas along the Texas border, known as *colonias,* over 35 percent of the residents are immigrants (Salinas 1988). The region also contains a disproportionately large Hispanic population. Over 80 percent of the people are Hispanic, largely of Mexican origin, in comparison to the state average of 26.3 percent (*Hispanic Children in Texas* 1995).

The communities in the United States along the Mexican border, particularly Texas, are undergoing significant social and economic transformations that have far-reaching implications for the well-being of children and families. For example, NAFTA is expected to have a major social impact on this part of the country by encouraging increased migration from the interior to the northern border part of Mexico and from Mexico to the United States. As a result, the U.S.–Mexico border presents unique problems for social service provision. Furthermore, deteriorating conditions, including the lack of basic public services, has led to the spread of communicable diseases and environmental degradation, which threaten the populations in both countries (Barry, Browne, and Sims 1994; "Down Mexico Way" 1992; Lorey 1993; Skolnick 1995a, 1995b).

The border region is already confronted with serious conditions that threaten the welfare of families. Poverty rates for the Texas border region reach alarming proportions. Overall, the child poverty rate in the border cities is 45.7 percent (ranging from 35 to 67 percent in every border county except two), compared to 21.3 percent in the rest of the state (*Hispanic Children in Texas* 1995). This means that in no other part of Texas is poverty so greatly concentrated than it is on the Mexican border. What's more, this area falls in the lower end on other indicators of well-being, experiencing unemployment rates as high as 34 percent and high school completion rates as low as 31 percent (*The State of Texas Children* 1994).

METHOD

The methodology for the study was based on a field-data gathering technique employed in public policy analysis and planning. It used an *elite* or *specialized* semi-structured interviewing method, "in which non-standardized information is collected by the analyst from selected, key individuals who have specialized knowledge of an event or process" (Patton and Sawicki 1993: 99). Three sites along the border in Texas were selected for the study: an urban, a semiurban, and a rural community. The three cities selected were, respectively, El Paso, Brownsville, and Eagle Pass. The type of information gathered around specific issues included a precise definition of the major problem, the context of the problem (including its historical background), predictions of trends, and information about the feasibility of policy preferences and alternatives. Focused group interviews allowed respondents to prioritize the main problems facing their communities.

FINDINGS

From the point of view of social workers and other service providers, the main findings indicate that issues facing the U.S.–Mexico border have an impact on social service provision at three levels: the family, the social service agency, and the community. First, service providers invariably identified poverty as the main problem in the border region in terms of its ramifications for all aspects of family life. Poverty, according to human service providers in South Texas, mainly affects children through the disruption that it creates within the family as manifested in terms of high rates of child abuse, juvenile delinquency, poor school outcomes, and mental health problems. Furthermore, in *colonias,* which are pockets of poverty unique to the border area, social, medical, and recreational services are virtually non-existent. As indicated earlier, immigrants tend to make up an important proportion of families living in *colonias.*

Second, at an agency level field interviews revealed that professionals have to grapple with the unique problems of service delivery along an international boundary. They emphasized, for example, that even though service providers from both the United States and Mexico wanted and attempted to collaborate, almost invariably their efforts failed to receive sanction (and funding) by the state and federal government. Yet people with problems of child abuse, juvenile delinquency, health, and so on, move between the two countries, and therefore follow-up services are required. The lack of such services often means that people return to the United States with problems that have escalated because of the lack of continuity of services. For example, a Mexican mother bears a child in the United States with a minor health problem, such as a vision problem, that is left untreated because the mother returns to Mexico and continuity of services is not ensured; the vision problem often surfaces again five years later as a learning disability when the child enters a U.S. border public school. Nevertheless, in spite of significant barriers, there is evidence of extensive informal collaboration between child welfare workers on both sides of the U.S.–Mexico international boundary (Daigle 1994). International collaboration between providers working with families who had members in both Mexico and the United States extended as far north as Los Angeles, California. However, such collaboration is based on interagency relationships or local agreements.

At the same time, these communities feel extremely isolated from the rest of the state, believing that the problems of the border area are often ignored or neglected and generally misunderstood. According to our interviews, the local border cities receive relatively low levels of funding from state and federal sources in comparison with other areas of the state for education, health, mental health, juvenile services, recreational facilities, and so on. This is true in part because funding formulas rely on population estimates for the area, and these estimates fail to include the number of people who live in Mexico but become involved in the social services system in the United States, such as youth who commit crimes in the United States or families who may have a child abuse problem that occurs in the United States. Because such persons are often members of families that reside in the United States, services are extended to them also. Court cases, such as *Edgewood v. Kirby* (1991), which addressed differential funding between school districts, have challenged this disparity in funding.

Two other agency-level issues for immigrants in the United States are the cross-utilization of social services and the existence of "binational families." Social workers report that services are provided to Mexican immigrants and residents on the Mexican border in the areas of child protective services and juvenile delinquency. However, although a number of studies related to the cross-border utilization of health services have been conducted (Chávez, Cornelius, and Jones 1985, Guendelman and Jasís 1992), formal research in the area of social services is needed. The other issue that poses a dilemma for social service providers is that of binational families, families who have some members who are documented immigrants and others who are in the United States illegally. According to Chávez (1992), many undocumented parents are reluctant to apply for benefits for their children for fear of being reported to the authorities.

Third, currently the most pressing concern of human service workers in the South Texas border region is the potential negative social impact of NAFTA on the community, an aspect that was neglected in the planning of NAFTA. Specifically, NAFTA is expected to generate rapid industrial and population growth, including large waves of migration from the southern part of Mexico to its northern border and subsequent immigration to the United States. Based on their direct contact with the community and their knowledge of social service delivery systems, providers recognize that they will not be able to offer adequate social, educational, and health services given existing resources.

Conclusion

Addressing the unique situation of immigrants from developing nations who live in the border communities of industrialized nations requires international collaboration in the formulation of human services policy. Yet, as we have seen, the possibilities for such a formulation are shaped by the political context within which human service providers operate. Traditionally the United States has lacked a comprehensive federal immigration policy related to immigrant entitlement and social assistance to ease assimilation. Current national policy has resulted in weak social supports for immigrants. Nevertheless, as shown in this article, social work theory suggests that international services to immigrants must incorporate a broader perspective, one that takes into account the immigrants' interconnections with their countries of origin. The analysis of the problems Mexican immigrants face on the U.S.–Mexico border presented in this article indicates that international collaboration between sending and receiving countries in the delivery of social services to immigrants is essential to effective social service provision. However, international collaboration does not necessarily call for the integration of the social welfare systems of the United States and Mexico or even a major reorganization of social service provision. For example, an analysis by Padilla and Daigle (1995) suggests that international cooperation in the area of social services can be achieved at the level of interagency links. Further research is needed to explore the prospects for international collaboration in the provision of social services in border communities.

Note

1. This research was conducted by the author as part of a larger policy study designed to inform policy makers of the problems facing Hispanic children and families in Texas with a special emphasis on the U.S.–Mexico border region. Laura Lein served as principal investigator for the study, which was funded by the Texas Department of Health, the Texas Department of Human Services, the Hogg Foundation for Mental Health, the RGK Foundation, and the Children's Trust Fund of Texas. Other parts of the study focused on health, education, and employment.

References

Aguilar, M. A. (in press). "Social Work Practice and Theory in Mexico." In D. Elliot, T. D. Watts, and N. S. Mayadas, eds., *International Handbook on Social Work Theory and Practice.* Westport, Conn.: Greenwood Press.

Ahearn, F. L., and J. L. Athey, eds. 1991. *Refugee Children: Theory, Research and Services.* Baltimore: Johns Hopkins University Press.

Asociación Fronteriza Mexicano-Estadounidense de Salud. 1990. *Proyecto consenso: Reporte final.* El Paso: Organización Panamericana de Salud.

Barry, T., H. Browne, and B. Sims. 1994. *Crossing the Line: Immigrants, Economic Integration, and Drug Enforcement on the U.S.–Mexico Border.* U.S.–Mexico Series, no. 3. Albuquerque: Resource Center Press.

Bean, F. D., J. Chapa, R. R. Berg, and K. A. Sowards. 1994. "Educational and Sociodemographic Incorporation among Hispanic Immigrants to the United States." In B. Edmonston and J. S. Passel, eds., *Immigration and Ethnicity: The Integration of America's Newest Arrivals.* Washington, D.C.: Urban Institute, pp. 73–100.

Center for Public Policy Priorities. 1996, August 14. "Analysis of Federal Welfare Reform." *Policy Page.*

Chávez, L. R. 1992. "Paradise at a Cost: The Incorporation of Undocumented Mexican Immigrants into a Local-Level Labor Market." In J. A. Bustamante, C. W. Reynolds, and R. A. Hinojosa Ojeda, eds., *U.S.–Mexico Relations: Labor Market Interdependence.* Stanford, Calif.: Stanford University Press, pp. 271–301.

Chávez, L. R., W. A. Cornelius, and O. W. Jones. 1985. "Mexican Immigrants and the Utilization of U.S. Health Services: The Case of San Diego," *Social Science Medicine* 21: 93–102.

Christensen, C. P. 1992. "Training for Cross-Cultural Social Work with Immigrants, Refugees, and Minorities: A Course Model." In A. S. Ryan, ed., *Social Work with Immigrants and Refugees.* New York: Haworth Press, pp. 79–97.

Daigle, L. 1994. *Child Welfare Service along the U.S.–Mexico Border: Efforts in Bi-National Cooperation.* Working paper no. 74. Austin: LBJ School of Public Affairs, University of Texas at Austin.

"Down Mexico Way." 1992, April 18. *Economist,* p. A24.

Drachman, D. 1992. "A Stage-of-Migration Framework for Service to Immigrant Populations." *Social Work* 37: 68–72.

Drachman, D., and A. Halberstadt, 1992. "A Stage-of-Migration Framework as Applied to Recent Soviet Emigres." In A. S. Ryan, ed., *Social Work with Immigrants and Refugees.* New York: Haworth Press, pp. 63–78.

Durán, C. R., R. C. Licea, and E. P. Duraza. 1994. *Sistemas de bienestar social en Norteamerica: Análisis comparado.* Mexico City: Imprenta Madero.

Edgewood Independent School District v. Kirby, 804 S.W. 2d 491 (Tex. 1991).

Estes, R. J., ed. 1992. *Internationalizing Social Work Education: A Guide to Resources for a New Century.* Philadelphia: Americor Press.

Fernández Franco, L. 1992. "Inmigración del tercer mundo y cooperación internacional en la Europa de los 90." In L. M. Ruiz and E. R. Lozano, eds., *Actas de las Terceras Jornadas Estatales sobre Perspectivas del Trabajo Social.* Granada: Escuela Universitaria de Trabajo Social, pp. 67–82.

Fix, M., and J. S. Passel, 1994. *Immigration and Immigrants: Setting the Record Straight.* Washington, D.C.: Urban Institute.

Guendelman, S., and M. A. Jasís. 1992. "Giving Birth across the Border: The San Diego–Tijuana Connection." *Social Science Medicine* 34: 419–425.

Hansen, N. 1983. "International Cooperation in Border Regions: An Overview and Research Agenda." *International Regional Science Review* 8: 255–270.

Healy, L. M. 1995. "Comparative and International Overview." In T. D. Watts, D. Elliot, and N. S. Mayadas, eds., *International Handbook on Social Work Education*. Westport, Conn.: Greenwood Press, pp. 421–439.

Herzog, L. A. 1985. "The Cross-Cultural Dimensions of Urban Land Use Policy on the U.S.–Mexico Border: A San Diego–Tijuana Case Study." *Social Science Journal* 22: 29–46.

Hispanic Children in Texas. 1995. Special Report of the Texas Kids Count Project, Center for Public Policy Priorities, and the School of Social Work, University of Texas at Austin. Austin: Texas Kids Count Project.

Hokenstad, M. C., S. K. Khinduka, and J. Midgley, eds. 1992. *Profiles in International Social Work*. Washington, D.C.: National Association of Social Workers Press.

Jacob, G. 1994. "Social Integration of Salvadoran Refugees." *Social Work* 39: 307–312.

Kelley, J. B., A. L. Balderrabano, and E. L. Briseño, 1986. "The Roles of Community Workers in the United States and Mexico." *Community Development Journal* 21: 11–22.

Le-Doux, C., and K. S. Stephens. 1992. "Refugee and Immigrant Social Service Delivery: Critical Management Issues." In A. S. Ryan, ed., *Social Work with Immigrants and Refugees*. New York: Haworth Press, pp. 31–45.

Leiper de Monchy, M. 1991. "Recovery and Rebuilding: The Challenge for Refugee Children and Service Providers." In F. L. Ahearn and J. L. Athey, eds., *Refugee Children: Theory, Research, and Services*. Baltimore: Johns Hopkins University Press, pp. 163–180.

Lorey, D. E., ed. 1993. *United States–Mexico Border Statistics since 1900: 1990 Update*. Los Angeles: Latin American Center Publications, University of California, Los Angeles.

Martínez, O. J. 1992. "Stages of Evolution in the History of the U.S.–Mexico Borderlands." In D. R. Abbott, ed., *Proceedings of the Forum "San Diego–Tijuana Borderlands: Problems and Prospects."* San Diego: Borderlands Project, San Diego Mesa College, pp. 9–13.

Midgley, J. 1990. "International Social Work." *Social Work* 35: 295–301.

————. 1992. "The Challenge of International Social Work." In M. C. Hokenstad, S. K. Khinduka, and J. Midgley, eds., *Profiles in International Social Work*. Washington, D.C.: National Association of Social Workers Press, pp. 13–27.

Padilla, Y. C., and L. Daigle. 1995. "Conceptualizing International Collaboration in Social Service Delivery in the U.S.–Mexico Border Region." Unpublished manuscript.

Patton, C., and P. Sawicki. 1993. *Basic Methods of Policy Analysis and Planning*. Englewood Cliffs, N.J.: Prentice-Hall.

Peralta, F. 1992. "Children of the Streets of Mexico." *Children and Youth Services Review* 14: 347–362.

Plascencia, F., and P. Wong. 1991. *Survey of Newly Legalized Persons in Texas: Executive Summary.* Austin: Center for the Study of Human Resources, LBJ School of Public Affairs, University of Texas at Austin.

Proposition 187. 1994. Illegal Aliens' Ineligibility for Public Services Verification and Reporting Initiative Statute, State of California.

Rolph, E. 1992. *Immigration Policies: Legacy from the 1980s and Issues for the 1990s.* Santa Monica, Calif.: Rand.

Rosenberg, D. E. 1991. "Serving America's Newcomers: States and Localities Are Taking the Lead in the Absence of a Comprehensive National Policy." *Public Welfare* 49: 28–37.

Ryan, A. S., ed. 1992. *Social Work with Immigrants and Refugees.* New York: Haworth Press.

Salinas, E. 1988. *The Colonias Factbook: A Survey of Living Conditions in Rural Areas of South Texas and West Texas Border Communities.* Austin: Texas Department of Human Services.

Schepps, D. 1994. "Brickmaking, Clean Air, and Binationalism: Environmental Cooperation on the U.S.–Mexico Border." *Institute of Latin American Studies Newsletter* (University of Texas at Austin) 28: 5.

Sherraden, M. D., and J. J. Martin. 1994. "Social Work with Immigrants: International Issues in Service Delivery." *International Social Work* 37: 369–384.

Skolnick, A. A. 1995a. "Along U.S. Southern Border, Pollution, Poverty, Ignorance, and Greed Threaten Nation's Health." *Journal of the American Medical Association* 273: 1479–1482.

———. 1995b. "Crossing Line on the Map in Search of Hope." *Journal of the American Medical Association* 273: 1646–1648.

The State of Texas Children 1994: A County-by-County Fact Book. 1994. Austin: Texas Kids Count Project.

Suárez y Toriello, E., and O. E. Chávez Alzaga. 1996. *Perfil de la frontera México–Estados Unidos.* Ciudad Juárez: Federación Mexicana de Asociaciones Privadas de Salud y Desarrollo Comunitario.

U.S. Bureau of the Census. 1993. *1990 Census of Population: Social and Economic Characteristics (Texas).* Washington, D.C.: U.S. Government Printing Office.

U.S.–Mexico Border Health Statistics. 1990. 6th ed., technical report no. #EP/PAHO/91/001. El Paso: Pan American Health Organization.

3

Providing Health Services to Immigrant and Refugee Populations in New York

Heike Thiel de Bocanegra and Francesca Gany

The proportion of immigrant groups in the United States varies by region. For example, while New York receives 60 percent of documented immigrants from the Dominican Republic and 70 percent of documented Guyanese immigrants, it receives less than 1 percent of documented Mexican immigrants, the largest immigrant group in the United States (see table 3.1). However, anecdotal evidence suggests that the number of undocumented Mexican immigrants coming directly from rural areas in Mexico to the New York metropolitan area has considerably increased in recent years. The diversity of New York's immigrant population creates complex challenges for the health care provider and planner, such as how to plan for divergent health risks, disease patterns, and health behaviors (Thiel de Bocanegra, Gany, and Fruchter 1993). Differences in access to health services may stem from differences in citizenship status, socioeconomic factors, years of residence in the United States, language, and culture (Gropper and Thiel de Bocanegra 1994).

The New York Task Force on Immigrant Health (NYTFIH), housed at the New York University School of Medicine, is a network of health care providers, social scientists, and community advocates working with immigrant and refugee communities in New York. The task force's goal is to increase access to health care and to ensure culturally appropriate quality health care for New York's immigrant and refugee groups. The increasing anti-immigrant sentiment in the United States and the corresponding policy changes provide a special challenge to this endeavor.

In 1994 residents of the state of California voted for a referendum, widely known as Proposition 187, that threatens to severely restrict or deny basic services such as health and education to undocumented immigrants. Section 130.(b) of this law states: "A person shall not receive any health care services from a publicly funded health care facility, to

Table 3.1. Immigrants by Selected Country of Birth: New York
City and the United States, 1982–1989

	Number NYC	Percent NYC	NYC as a Percentage of the U.S.
All Immigrants	684,819	100.0	14.5
Dominican Republic	115,759	16.9	60.8
Jamaica	72,343	10.6	44.5
China	71,881	10.5	20.1
Guyana	53,638	7.8	70.2
Haiti	40,819	6.0	37.4
Colombia	22,805	3.3	26.7
Korea	20,112	2.9	7.4
India	20,039	2.9	9.7
Ecuador	17,930	2.6	49.9
Philippines	13,539	2.0	3.6
Mexico	3,144	0.5	0.6

Source: Annual Immigrant Tape Files, 1982–1989, U.S. Immigration and Naturalization Service. Cited in New York City Department of Planning 1992.

which he or she is otherwise entitled until the legal status of that person has been verified as one of the following: (1) A citizen of the United States, (2) An alien lawfully admitted as a permanent resident, and (3) An alien lawfully admitted for a temporary period of time." Section 48215.(a) states: "No public elementary or secondary school shall admit, or permit the attendance of, any child who is not a citizen of the United States, an alien lawfully admitted as a permanent resident, or a person who is otherwise authorized under federal law to be present in the United States."

This proposition is now being challenged in court. In New York the so-called Spirit of Proposition 187 bills (S. 3089, 3090, 3091, 3092, and 3093) were presented to the New York State Senate. These initiatives reflect the erroneous perception of many persons that immigrants come to the United States to take advantage of the welfare system and end up being a burden to society. On the contrary, immigrants are generally very healthy and tend to have rates of health service utilization below those of the general U.S. population (Chávez, Cornelius, and Jones 1985). Foreign-born women have better birth outcomes than U.S.-born women when controlling for socioeconomic status (Cabral et al. 1990). The utilization of preventive health services such as general checkups and dental services is very low for immigrants because of language and systemic access barriers. This may result in higher utilization rates of emergency care (Chávez, Cornelius, and Jones 1985, Chávez, Flores, and Lopes-Garza 1992) and a higher likelihood that the diagnosis of preventable diseases is unnecessarily delayed (Fruchter et al. 1986, Fruchter et al. 1985).

The NYTFIH has developed a multifaceted approach to help immigrant populations. This approach builds upon the ecological framework by developing programs which target policy makers, the health care system, the community, health care providers, and individual immigrants, respectively. In the following text, two projects that exemplify the task force's approach will be described. These projects were developed to address two of the main components of effective health care for immigrants: ensuring access to care and ensuring culturally appropriate quality care.

Ensuring Access to Care: The Tuberculosis Community Outreach, Education, and Screening Project

Tuberculosis rates in the United States have increased by 20 percent since 1985. Foreign-born persons constitute 60 percent of the total increase in the United States (Centers for Disease Control 1990). The incidence of tuberculosis is considerably higher for ethnic minorities living in larger cities such as New York City than for those living elsewhere in the United States (Centers for Disease Control 1987). Foreign-born individuals are at risk to develop active tuberculosis because (1) they come from endemic countries, (2) they may have precarious living conditions, and (3) they may postpone the utilization of health care, except in cases of emergencies. The lack of contact with the health care system may impede the detection of tuberculosis infection and the possibility of preventing the development of active tuberculosis with prophylactic treatment with isoniazid (INH prophylaxis).

The NYTFIH developed outreach strategies to reach immigrants who are not likely to be in contact with the health care system. Outreach strategies vary by immigrant group. For example, many Haitians can be reached through established community groups such as churches, while outreach to immigrants from West Africa is conducted mainly one-on-one, visiting them in single-room occupancy hotels or talking to them on the street (many of the West African immigrants are street vendors).

These strategies integrate tuberculosis education into immigrants' priorities, such as getting immigration status for themselves, sponsoring family members, obtaining financial stability, and learning English. Community-based organizations (CBOs) are particularly influential in these matters because they have the trust of and access to the various communities. The NYTFIH works with CBOs to include tuberculosis education and screening in their programs. Bicultural and bilingual outreach workers who are identified and hired by CBOs are trained to educate immigrants on tuberculosis and administer the Mantoux test at places such as not-for-profit organizations and churches that provide job training and placement, legal counseling, or English-as-a-second-language (ESL) classes. In the first year, this CBO outreach focused on immigrants and refugees from Haiti, Africa, the former Soviet Republic, and South Asia. In 1995 the program was expanded to Latino immigrants (Dominicans, Ecuadoreans, Mexicans, and Colombians).

Simultaneously, the task force works with the health care community to provide fast entry into the health care system. Clients who have a positive PPD-Mantoux skin test result, which means that they are infected by TB germs, are referred to the health care facility to receive chest X-rays and are counseled to receive preventive INH therapy. The outreach workers maintain close contact with their clients to ensure that immigrants do not get lost in one of the steps of tuberculosis diagnosis and preventive treatment.

Of the 826 persons who were tested from September 1994 to July 1995, 58 percent had no health insurance, 12 percent did not have any formal schooling, 66 percent had never had a PPD skin test, 5 percent of those who said they had a previous PPD test did not know the results, and 8.4 percent did not return to find out the reading of the test. Of the 816 who returned, 40 percent were PPD positive (see table 3.2).

Through tuberculosis outreach and activities, fourteen persons with active tuberculosis were identified. They are from a variety of countries: Haiti (3), Senegal (3), Mauritania (2), Ivory Coast (2), Guinea (2), Zaire (1), and Burundi (1). Two thirds of them had lived in the United States for less than two years. Half of them did not have any health insurance, six were on Medicaid (the federal insurance that covers low-income persons and refugees for nine months after arrival), and one person had private insurance. Four of the fourteen active tuberculosis cases had never had a PPD test before.

Systematic outreach to recent arrivals, including those who do not have any insurance, might have prevented some or all of these active tu-

Table 3.2. TB Outreach and Screening in New York City:
Participant Characteristics (percentages)

	Yes	No
PPD+ (infected with TB)	40	60
Had health insurance	42	58
Had at least one year of formal schooling	88	12
Have had a previous PPD[a]	34	66

Note: N = 826. No-show rate and incomplete data = 8.4 percent.

a. Of these, 5 percent did not know the results.

berculosis cases. Because of this, the task force will expand this program
to other immigrant groups and to other geographic locations beyond
New York City.

Culturally Appropriate Care:
Immigrant Health Training

What happens to immigrants when they first enter the health care system? If immigrants feel misunderstood or discriminated against, the first
contact with the health care system may be the last for a long time. Prenatal and pediatric care are windows of opportunity to reach new arrivals who otherwise may not go to the doctor and to encourage them to
seek preventive and early health care for themselves and their children.
One important effort the NYTFIH makes to improve the system is to
train health care providers on cross-cultural health care issues. The training was developed to be offered on-site to all staff members at maternal
child health facilities, including clerical staff. It is often the intake clerk
who has the first contact with the patient and can make the patient feel
very uncomfortable.

The immigrant health training is based on adult education principles
such as building upon the participants' knowledge and experiences and
presenting the content in a problem-posing way. Cultural sensitivity is
presented as part of a general understanding of immigrants' sociocultural context and its impact on health care behaviors. The modules address language barriers and how to work with interpreters, entitlements
and legal issues, previous experiences with the health care system, and
the influences of culture on health care practices and provider-patient

interaction (Gany and Thiel de Bocanegra 1996). Once rapport is established with the trainees, more sensitive and potentially threatening topics such as values, beliefs and practices, and provider biases are discussed.

One part of the training is the provision of epidemiological information on maternal child health to change some misperceptions about immigrants. For example, foreign-born women in the United States have better birth outcomes than U.S.-born women, when controlling for socioeconomic level (Cabral et al. 1990). In New York City, the percentage of teenage mothers and the percentage of women who receive late prenatal care (after six months of pregnancy) are greater among Hispanic women born on the U.S. mainland than among Puerto Rican–born women and non–Puerto Rican Hispanic Caribbean women (Chavkin, Busner, and McLauglin 1987). Also, the infant mortality rate from 1980 to 1983 was higher among children of U.S.-born Hispanic mothers than among children of Puerto Rican–born or Hispanic Caribbean women (Chavkin, Busner, and McLauglin 1987). Immigrant women are less likely to smoke or use alcohol during pregnancy. However, these healthy behaviors deteriorate after arrival to the United States. In other words, migration to the United States and acculturation to perceived U.S. values can have a detrimental effect on health. In the immigrant health training, providers are encouraged to identify immigrants' resources and ways to enable immigrants to remain healthy.

Implications for a Culturally Appropriate Project Methodology

The NYTFIH's aim is to develop a methodology of collaboration with community-based organizations and intervention at the provider and health care level. This methodology includes developing flexibility to serve newly arriving groups, identifying the community structure of immigrant groups and their leaders, developing a participatory approach in education and outreach, monitoring immigrants' disease patterns through improved health statistics, and promoting research activities on immigrant health.

DEVELOPING FLEXIBILITY TO SERVE NEWLY ARRIVING GROUPS

Newly arriving groups represent a variety of epidemiologic profiles and health beliefs and practices. In both programs, the tuberculosis project and the immigrant health training, the most recent immigrant groups required special attention in the project design and implementation. Eleven of the fourteen persons with active tuberculosis came from African countries that are not large sending countries to the United States. Also, at the immigrant health training sessions, providers asked us to talk about recent groups, not the largest groups. For example, at one site 80 percent of the patients are Hispanic. The staff felt competent in dealing with Latino culture and living conditions. However, they expressed the need to learn more about Bengali patients because these patients had recently started to attend the clinic in large numbers and their health behaviors and family interactions were perceived as being very different and unfamiliar.

IDENTIFYING THE COMMUNITY STRUCTURE OF IMMIGRANT GROUPS AND THEIR LEADERS

The challenge in targeting newly arriving groups is that they often lack a clear community structure and may not yet have a community support system. They may contain many undocumented residents, who may fear deportation when accessing social and health services. It is therefore important to design programs that allow the development of working relationships with newly arriving groups as soon as possible. The identification of key leaders, decision-making structures, and local resources can be done through local community assessments that capture the needs and strengths of the immigrant communities and identify commonalities and differences among immigrant groups.

DEVELOPING A PARTICIPATORY APPROACH IN EDUCATION AND OUTREACH

The involvement of the community in program planning, implementation, and evaluation at every intervention level is essential for the design of culturally appropriate health programs. Community participation has permitted the development of tuberculosis outreach models that meet the needs of diverse language and cultural groups. Trainees in educational activities, for example the providers in the immigrant health training, can be involved through a needs assessment prior to the training and through learner-centered methodologies.

MONITORING IMMIGRANTS' DISEASE PATTERNS THROUGH IMPROVED HEALTH STATISTICS

Health statistics that divide by racial and ethnic categories without determining country of birth and length of stay, for example, do not capture New York's diversity and are meaningless for culturally appropriate program planning. For example, a Black person living in New York City can be U.S.-born, from Jamaica (speaking English), from Haiti (speaking Creole), or from the Dominican Republic (speaking Spanish), to list just a few of the possibilities. In part because of the efforts of the New York Task Force on Immigrant Health, several health care facilities in New York have included measures on country of birth or language proficiency in their routine medical intake and encounter forms.

PROMOTING RESEARCH ACTIVITIES ON IMMIGRANT HEALTH

Research activities should identify factors that impede or facilitate healthy behaviors, such as breast feeding or low smoking rates, and those that avoid the negative impact of acculturation. New York's diversity also permits comparative research across immigrant groups that are affected by the same health promotion policies. Through comparative research projects, such as projects comparing immigrants' experiences in different countries and/or regions, it will be possible to identify risk factors that affect immigrants and to develop appropriate intervention strategies. These should be combined with the development of community assessment tools for the identification of disease prevalence and health care–seeking patterns.

These five components should be part of any public health effort that targets immigrant and refugee populations. A methodology for health care and social service providers who serve migrant populations has to take into account that, while recent arrivals are often the groups in most need and with fewer defined community structures, they are most likely to be overseen and neglected. Epidemiologists and health service researchers have to continuously question the accuracy and validity of their indicators to identify new arrivals. For example, country-of-birth information may be an insufficient identifier for an African migrant group with strong regional or tribal characteristics. Providers have to determine the needs and strengths of recent arrivals and evaluate the appropriateness of their educational and service strategies. Culturally appropriate programs can only be developed with the active involvement of the community in planning, decision making, implementation, and monitoring. The development of comprehensive and participatory programs will ultimately ensure effective quality care to immigrant and refugee populations.

References

Cabral, H., L. Fried, S. Levenson, H. Amaro, and B. Zuckerman. 1990. "Foreign-Born and U.S.-Born Black Women: Differences in Health Behaviors and Birth Outcomes." *American Journal of Public Health* 80: 70–72.

Centers for Disease Control. 1987. *Tuberculosis in the United States.* DHHS publication no. (CDC) 89-8322. Atlanta: CDC.

———. 1990. "Tuberculosis among Foreign-Born Persons Entering the United States." *Morbidity and Mortality Weekly Report* 39, RR-18.

Chávez, L., W. Cornelius, and O. Jones. 1985. "Mexican Immigrants and the Utilization of U.S. Health Services: The Case of San Diego." *Social Sciences and Medicine* 21: 3–102.

Chávez, L., E. Flores, and M. Lopes-Garza. 1992. "Undocumented Latin American Immigrants and U.S. Health Services: An Approach to a Political Economy of Utilization." *Medical Anthropology Quarterly* 6: 6–26.

Chavkin, W., C. Busner, and M. McLauglin. 1987. "Reproductive Health: Caribbean Women in New York City, 1980–1984." *International Migration Review* 21: 609–625.

Fruchter, R., J. Remy, W. Burnett, and J. Boyce. 1986. "Cervical Cancer in Immigrant Caribbean Women." *American Journal of Public Health* 76: 797–799.

Fruchter, R., C. Wright, B. Habenstreit, J. Remy, J. Boyce, and P. Imperato. 1985. "Screening for Cervical and Breast Cancer among Caribbean Immigrants." *Journal of Community Health* 10: 121–135.

Gany, F., and H. Thiel de Bocanegra. 1996. "Maternal-Child Immigrant Health Training: Changing Knowledge and Attitudes to Improve Health Care Delivery." *Patient Education and Counseling* 27: 23–31.

Gropper, R., and H. Thiel de Bocanegra. 1994. "Health Beliefs and Practices across Cultures." In H. Thiel de Bocanegra, ed., *Integrated Maternal Child Immigrant Health Care for Immigrant and Refugee Populations* (conference proceedings). New York: New York Task Force on Immigrant Health, pp. 24–34.

New York City Department of Planning. 1992. *The Newest New Yorkers: An Analysis of Immigration into New York City during the 1980s.* New York: Department of Planning.

Thiel de Bocanegra, H., F. Gany, and R. Fruchter. 1993. "Available Epidemiologic Data on New York's Latino Population: A Critical Review of the Literature." *Ethnicity and Disease* 3: 413–426.

4

Perinatal Outcomes of North African Immigrants in Belgium

Pierre Buekens, Thérèse Delvaux, Isabelle Godin,
Godelieve Masuy-Stroobant, and Sophie Alexander

In several countries of continental Europe, the most numerous groups of non-European immigrants originate from North Africa (Algeria, Morocco, and Tunisia). In Belgium in 1987, 3.7 percent of mothers were North Africans (Masuy-Stroobant, Buekens, and Gourbin 1992). This differs from the situation in the United Kingdom, where non-European immigrants are mainly from Asia, the Caribbean, and sub-Saharan Africa (Macfarlane and Mugford 1984). Contrary to studies from the United Kingdom, many migrant studies from other European countries have been published in local journals and often in languages other than English. They are not widely cited in the international literature, though many of these publications present results that are different from the British ones.

This paper reviews available data on birth outcomes of North African immigrants in Belgium. We have also reviewed publications from other European countries and from Algeria, Morocco, and Tunisia.

Birthweight

In Belgium, North African immigrants are mostly from Morocco (Attar 1992). Birthweight is registered on birth certificates in Belgium, which is not the case in France and the Netherlands (Alexander et al. 1995, Gourbin and Masuy-Stroobant 1995). Surprisingly, there are fewer low-birthweight newborns among North Africans than among Belgians (Buekens, Cleries Escayola, and Derom 1990). Table 4.1 shows data from 1983 single birth and death certificates. The low-birthweight rate among North Africans was only 3.9 percent. This was unexpected in a population of low socioeconomic status: 88.3 percent of husbands of North African mothers were manual workers in 1983, while this was the case for only 43.1 percent of Belgian mothers (Buekens, Cleries Escayola, and Derom 1990). Other Belgian studies did not separate North Africans from Turks or Greeks but also reported that migrant groups including many North Africans had few low-birthweight newborns. A survey of live births and stillbirths occurring in one Belgian province in 1979–80 reported reduced low-birthweight rates among Greeks, Turks, and North African newborns (5.9 percent) compared with Belgian newborns (6.4 percent) (Masuy-Stroobant 1988). An analysis of 1981–84 birth and death certificates showed that Moroccan and Turkish newborns had heavier birthweights than newborns from the European Community (see figure 4.1) (Peeters and Van Der Veen 1989, 1990). In summary, all Belgian results support the idea that North Africans have few low-birthweight newborns.

Similar results were reported in the Netherlands (Doornbos and Nordbeck 1985, Doornbos et al. 1991). Data about singletons collected between 1972 and 1982 in three hospitals in Amsterdam showed low-birthweight rates of 5.8 percent among Moroccan and Turkish newborns and 7.3 percent among Dutch newborns (Doornbos and Nordbeck 1985, Doornbos et al. 1991). Lower rates of low-birthweight infants among the Moroccan and Turkish population than among the Dutch one were still observed after stratification by age, parity, maternal height, and maternal weight (Doornbos and Nordbeck 1985).

In France, most North African immigrants are from Algeria. Population-based data are from the 1972, 1976, and 1981 French National Natality Surveys (Kaminski et al. 1978, Saurel-Cubizolles, Rabarison, and Rumeau-Rouquette 1984, Saurel-Cubizolles et al. 1986). The analysis of the surveys generally compared women with North African nationality (Algerian, Moroccan, and Tunisian) who were born in North Africa on the one hand, and women with French nationality who were born in France on the other hand. In 1972 the low-birthweight rate was 10 percent among newborns of North African origin and 6 percent among French newborns (Saurel-Cubizolles et al. 1986). In 1981 the National Natality Survey reported no statistically significant difference in low-birthweight rates between newborns whose mothers were from North Africa (7 percent) or from France (5 percent) (Saurel-Cubizolles et al. 1986). A study performed in 1963–69 in twelve maternity units in Paris reported frequencies of newborns weighing less than 2,501g of 7 percent among North Africans and of 6 percent among the French population

Table 4.1. Low-Birthweight and Perinatal Mortality Rates among Singletons: Birth and Death Certificates, Belgium, 1983

Nationality	Birthweight < 2,500g		Perinatal Mortality	
	n	%	*n*	per 1,000
Belgium	(100,590)	5.2	(100,769)	10.7
EC[a] North	(2,622)	5.3	(2,624)	6.9
EC[a] South	(3,899)	5.9	(3,903)	9.0
North Africa	(4,388)	3.9	(4,402)	14.8
Turkey	(2,135)	4.4	(2,141)	17.7

Source: Buekens, Cleries Escayola, and Derom 1990.

a. European Community.

(Kaminski, Goujard, and Rumeau-Rouquette 1975). Another hospital-based study reported lower frequencies of babies weighing less than 2,800g among immigrants from North Africa (11.3 percent) than among French newborns (14.6 percent) (Dumont and Boyaud 1978).

Reduced low-birthweight rates have been observed in North Africa (see table 4.2). The World Health Organization estimated that in 1990 the low-birthweight rates were 9 percent in Algeria and Morocco and 8 percent in Tunisia (Maternal Health and Safe Motherhood Programme 1992). This was lower than the African average and less than half of the estimated low-birthweight rate for developing countries. The data used by the World Health Organization to derive estimates for Algeria and Morocco were from United Nations statistics or unpublished documents. For Tunisia, part of the information was from published studies that reported low-birthweight rates ranging from 6.7 percent to 10 percent (Milliez, Ghorbel, and Rerik 1980, Khrouf et al. 1982, Marrekchi et al. 1986, Soltani et al. 1991).

Other Tunisian studies provided estimated low-birthweight rates of less than 10 percent (Beghin and Jerfal 1973, De Schampeleire, Parent, and Chatteur 1980, Gueddana, Ben Aïcha, and Jarraya 1989). One of these studies concerned a 1984–85 representative sample of births (Gueddana, Ben Aïcha, and Jarraya 1989). Birthweight data were available for 4,601 newborns, corresponding to 54 percent of all births included in the study. Among the 4,601 newborns, 363 (7.9 percent) had a birthweight

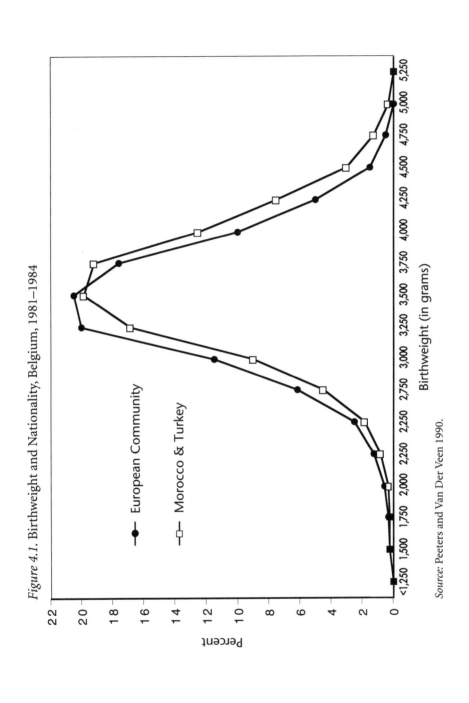

Figure 4.1. Birthweight and Nationality, Belgium, 1981–1984

● European Community

□ Morocco & Turkey

Percent

Birthweight (in grams)

<22 20 18 16 14 12 10 8 6 4 2 0

<1,250 1,500 1,750 2,000 2,250 2,500 2,750 3,000 3,250 3,500 3,750 4,000 4,250 4,500 4,750 5,000 5,250

Source: Peeters and Van Der Veen 1990.

lower than 2,501g, and 466 (10.1 percent) had a birthweight of 4,000g or more. The proportion of newborns weighing less than 2,501g was lower in urban areas (7.3 percent) than in rural areas (9.1 percent).

Another study of 250 single newborns performed in Cap Bon, Tunisia, reported a low-birthweight rate of 5.6 percent (De Schampeleire, Parent, and Chatteur 1980). The study provided data on weight for gestational age measured according to the Dubowitz score. The proportion of large-for-date infants was 22 percent. These infants were above the 90th percentile of the Lubchenco weight for gestational age curves. This is in agreement with a study performed in Tunis, Tunisia, which also found that 22 percent of infants were large-for-date (Khrouf et al. 1982). Nutritional factors have been suggested as a possible explanation. De Schampeleire, Parent, and Chatteur (1980) cite unpublished studies of dietary habits showing that the daily diet in Tunisia has a high carbohydrate content. In another Tunisian study, one hundred pregnant women answered a twenty-four-hour nutritional recall questionnaire (Siala Gaïgi et al. 1990). The results showed that thirty women were eating more than 2,500 kcal. per day.

A study performed in Ceuta, a Spanish territory on the Moroccan coast, compared newborns of Moroccan origin with newborns of Spanish origin (Martínez Cortés et al. 1992). Only singletons born at term (38–42 weeks) were included. The mean birthweight of newborns of Moroccan origin was 3,428g, and the mean birthweight of the Spanish-origin group was 3,280g. After the exclusion of smokers, the mean birthweights were 3,430g and 3,318g, respectively. Birthweights remained high among infants of Moroccan origin after stratification for parity.

That few low birthweights were reported among babies born in North Africa suggests that the low-birthweight rates observed among North Africans born in Europe are probably not the result of a "healthy migrant effect." Such a selection effect was described by Marmot, Adelstein, and Bulusu (1984), who pointed out that migrants could be healthier than compatriots who did not migrate.

Data from Israel also showed that infants of North African origin have higher birthweights than infants of other ethnic groups (Yudkin, Harlap, and Baras 1983). Birthweight was higher if the mother had immigrated from North Africa to Israel after the age of ten years than if she had immigrated at a younger age or had been born in Israel. This suggests that environmental and cultural factors played a role in the observed birthweight distributions.

Table 4.2. Estimated Low-Birthweight Frequencies, 1990
(percentages)

Country or Region	Low Birthweight
Europe	6
Belgium	6
Africa	15
Algeria	9
Morocco	9
Tunisia	8
Developing countries	19

Source: Maternal Health and Safe Motherhood Program 1992.

Preterm Deliveries

Many North African women don't know the date of their last menstrual period (Buekens et al. 1984, Saurel-Cubizolles et al. 1986, Stengel, Saurel-Cubizolles, and Kaminski 1986). Those who ignore their last menstrual period might be at risk of having poor perinatal outcomes (Buekens et al. 1984). It is thus difficult to compare the frequency of preterm deliveries among different populations.

Belgian national data from 1983 birth and death certificates show that the frequency of preterm (less than 37 completed weeks of gestational age) single deliveries was 4.4 percent among North Africans and 4.6 percent among Belgians (Buekens, Cleries Escayola, and Derom 1990). In the Netherlands, Doornbos and Nordbeck (1985) reported frequencies of preterm single deliveries of 9.9 percent among Moroccan and Turkish women and 6.7 percent among Dutch women. Adjusting for age, parity, and maternal weight and height did not change the results in a significant way.

In France, data from the 1972 National Natality Survey show a higher preterm delivery rate among North African women (19 percent) than among French women (8 percent) (Saurel-Cubizolles et al. 1986). Such a difference was not observed in the 1981 survey: the preterm rate was 8 percent among North African women and 5 percent among French women. Hospital-based studies reported conflicting results. Some authors observed higher preterm rates among immigrants from North Africa than among French women (Kaminski, Goujard, and Rumeau-Rouquette 1975, Dumont and Boyaud 1978). Others found low preterm or prematurity rates among immigrants from North Africa (Berger, Laugier, and Soutoul 1974, Blanc 1980, Adrai et al. 1985, Berardi, Benslama, and Alexandre 1988).

The frequency of preterm deliveries in North African countries is difficult to estimate. Some hospital-based data are available and most suggest that preterm rates are relatively low. In Morocco, Boutaleb et al. (1982) found a preterm rate of 4.4 percent in Casablanca. In Tunisia, preterm rates of 3.2 percent and 4.7 percent have been reported (Khrouf et al. 1982, Soltani et al. 1991), but De Schampeleire, Parent, and Chatteur (1980) found a preterm rate of 20.8 percent.

Perinatal Mortality

Belgian data from 1974–75 showed that perinatal mortality was higher among babies born to North African mothers compared with babies born to Belgian mothers (Masuy-Stroobant, Loriaux, and Gerard 1979; Masuy-Stroobant 1984, 1987). An excess of mortality among North Africans was also shown in 1983 (table 4.1), and in pooled analyses of 1981–84 data (Peeters and Van Der Veen 1989, 1990) and 1980–87 data (Masuy-Stroobant, Buekens, and Gourbin 1992). This high mortality was observed despite their high birthweight, suggesting that birthweight-specific mortality is high among North Africans.

In the Netherlands, Doornbos et al. (1991) did not observe an increased perinatal mortality among Moroccan and Turkish immigrants in their study performed in three hospitals in Amsterdam. A case-control study of perinatal deaths that occurred in Amsterdam and the Hague between 1975 and 1980 showed a slightly increased risk of perinatal death among Moroccans and Turks (Nijhuis, Nordbeck, and Belleman 1985). However, another study from Amsterdam showed that underregistration of perinatal deaths was more common among Moroccan and Turkish immigrants than among the Dutch population (Doornbos, Nordbeck, and Treffers 1987).

In France, data from the 1972 and 1981 National Natality Surveys showed higher stillbirth rates among women of North African origin compared with French women (Kaminski et al. 1978, Saurel-Cubizolles et al. 1986). Data from birth and death certificates from 1981 also showed an increased stillbirth rate when the nationality of the father was Algerian, Moroccan, or Tunisian (13.6 per thousand) compared with newborns having a French father (7.2 per thousand) (Saurel-Cubizolles et al. 1986).

A Paradigm Shift

A widely accepted paradigm is that populations of low socioeconomic status have many low-birthweight newborns. It is thus to be expected that immigrants with low socioeconomic status should have high frequencies of low-birthweight newborns. This is true in the United Kingdom (Macfarlane and Mugford 1984). However, we reported that the vast majority of available data show that North African immigrants in Belgium and in other countries have few low-birthweight newborns. In the United States, Mexican migrants born in Mexico also have few low-birthweight babies (Guendelman et al. 1990). These observations are challenging our traditional views on low-birthweight epidemiology.

Differences in nutrition, smoking, or social support networks are mechanisms that could possibly explain the reduced frequency of low-birthweight newborns and the high birthweight of North African immigrants. Future studies should attempt to document these environmental factors. Other studies should be focused on access to and quality of care. Their objective should be to explain why North African immigrants have a high perinatal mortality despite their adequate birthweight.

References

Adrai, J., B. Blanc, H. Ruf, S. Dupont, M. Conte, and J. P. Delpont. 1985. "La grossesse et l'accouchement de la Nord-Africaine." *Revue Française de Gynécologie et Obstétrique* 80: 703–705.

Alexander, S., M. Boutsen, F. Kittel, and P. Buekens. 1995. "Erreurs et discordances dans l'enregistrement du taux d'insuffisance pondérale en Europe." *Revue d'Epidémiologie et de Santé Publique* 43: 272–280.

Attar, R. 1992. "Historique de l'immigration maghrébine en Belgique." In A. Morelli, ed. *Histoire des étrangers et de l'immigration en Belgique de la préhistoire à nos jours.* Brussels: Editions Vie Ouvrière, pp. 290–310.

Beghin, D., and I. Jerfal. 1973. "Le poids de naissance des nouveau-nés de la ville de Grombalia, Cap Bon." *Archives de l'Institut Pasteur de Tunis* 50: 239–242.

Berardi, J. C., F. Benslama, and B. Alexandre. 1988. "La prévention communautaire de la prématurité: Étude dans une communauté de migrantes maghrébines." *Journal de Gynécologie Obstétrique et Biologie de la Reproduction* 17: 851–859.

Berger, C., J. Laugier, and J. H. Soutoul. 1974. "Caractéristiques de l'accouchement et du nouveau-né de migrante: Étude de 800 dossiers." *Journal de Gynécologie Obstétrique et Biologie de la Reproduction* 3: 1227–1234.

Blanc, B. 1980. "Grossesse et accouchement chez la Nord-Africaine immigrée." *Revue Française de Gynécologie et Obstétrique* 75: 281–286.

Boutaleb, Y., N. Lahlou, A. Outghiri, and M. Mesbahi. 1982. "Le poids de naissance dans un pays africain." *Journal de Gynécologie Obstétrique et Biologie de la Reproduction* 11: 68–72.

Buekens, P., M. Cleries Escayola, and R. Derom. 1990. "Perinatal Outcomes of Immigrants in Belgium." *Archives of Public Health* 48: 33–40.

Buekens, P., P. Delvoye, E. Wollast, and C. Robyn. 1984. "Epidemiology of Pregnancies with Unknown Last Menstrual Period." *Journal of Epidemiology and Community Health* 38: 79–80.

De Schampeleire, I., M. A. Parent, and C. Chatteur. 1980. "Excessive Carbohydrate Intake in Pregnancy and Neonatal Obesity: Study in Cap Bon, Tunisia." *Archives of Diseases of Childhood* 55: 521–526.

Doornbos, J. P. R., and H. J. Nordbeck. 1985. "Perinatal Mortality: Obstetric Factors in a Community of Mixed Ethnic Origin in Amsterdam." Doctoral diss., University of Amsterdam.

Doornbos, J. P. R., H. J. Nordbeck, and P. E. Treffers. 1987. "The Reliability of Perinatal Mortality Statistics in the Netherlands." *American Journal of Obstetrics and Gynecology* 156: 1183–1187.

Doornbos, J. P. R., H. J. Nordbeck, A. E. Van Enk, A. S. Muller, and P. E. Treffers. 1991. "Differential Birthweights and the Clinical Relevance of Birthweight Standards in a Multiethnic Society." *International Journal of Obstetrics and Gynecology* 34: 319–324.

Dumont, M., and M. Boyaud. 1978. "La grossesse et l'accouchement chez les femmes migrantes." *Journal Médical de Lyon* 59: 35–47.

Gourbin, C., and G. Masuy-Stroobant. 1995. "Registration of Vital Data: Are Live Births and Stillbirths Comparable All over Europe?" *Bulletin of the World Health Organization* 73: 449–460.

Gueddana, N., N. Ben Aïcha, and S. Jarraya. 1989. *Un enfant et deux Tunisies: Enquête nationale sur la mortalité et la morbidité infantiles.* Tunis: Ministère de la Santé Publique.

Guendelman, S., J. B. Gould, M. Hudes, and B. Eskenazi. 1990. "Generational Differences in Perinatal Health among the Mexican American Population: Findings from HHANES 1982–84." *American Journal of Public Health* 80 (supplement): 61–65.

Kaminski, M., B. Blondel, G. Bréart, M. Franc, and C. du Mazaubrun. 1978. "Issue de la grossesse et surveillance prénatale chez les femmes migrantes." *Revue d'Epidémiologie et de Santé Publique* 26: 29–46.

Kaminski, M., J. Goujard, and C. Rumeau-Rouquette. 1975. "La grossesse des femmes migrantes à Paris." *Revue Française de Gynécologie et Obstétrique* 70: 483–491.

Khrouf, N., S. Ben Becher, R. Brauner, M. N. Chaabouni, and B. Hamza. 1982. "Développement fetal du nouveau-né tunisien en zone urbaine: Études prospectives sur 1035 naissances." *Annales de Pédiatrie* 29: 602–606.

Macfarlane, A., and M. Mugford. 1984. "Birth Counts: Statistics of Pregnancy and Childbirth." London: Her Majesty's Stationery Office.

Marmot, M. G., A. M. Adelstein, and L. Bulusu. 1984. "Lessons from the Study of Immigrants' Mortality." *Lancet* 1: 1455–1457.

Marrekchi, R., A. Rerik, S. Rerik, R. Rerik, A. Fourati, F. Marrekchi, A. Ghorbel, and A. Triki. 1986. "Facteurs de risque de l'hypotrophie foetale (Étude retrospective à la maternité de Sfax)." *La Tunisie Médicale* 64: 587–591.

Martínez Cortés, F., M. V. Martínez Guerrero, P. Valdivielso Felices, J. R. Legros Carrenard, and J. Martín Sánchez. 1992. "Valores antropométricos en el recién nacido: Estudio comparativo en dos grupos étnicos." *Anales Españoles de Pediatría* 37: 399–401.

Masuy-Stroobant, G. 1984. *Les déterminants de la mortalité infantile: La Belgique d'hier et d'aujourd'hui.* Louvain-la-Neuve, Belgium: Ciaco.

———. 1987. "Pour une identification des familles à risque: Les décès infantiles en Belgique en 1974–1975." *Archives Belges de Médecine Sociale, Hygiène, Médecine du Travail et Médecine Légale* 45: 1–30.

———. 1988. "Santé de l'enfant et inégalités sociales: Une enquête dans le Hainaut sur le comportement préventif des mères." *Rapport Poliwa* 3. Louvain-la-Neuve, Belgium: Ciaco.

Masuy-Stroobant, G., P. Buekens, and C. Gourbin. 1992. "Perinatal Health in Belgium 1980–1987." *Archives of Public Health* 50: 217–239.

Masuy-Stroobant, G., M. Loriaux, and H. Gerard. 1979. "Mort ou survie à la naissance?" *Rapport Poliwa* 2. Brussels: Centre d'Étude de la Population et de la Famille.

Maternal Health and Safe Motherhood Program. 1992. *Low Birth Weight: A Tabulation of Available Information.* WHO/MCH/92.2. Geneva and New York: World Health Organization and UNICEF.

Milliez, J., A. Ghorbel, and S. Rerik. 1980. "Activité de la maternité de Sfax de 1976–1978: A propos de 20000 accouchements." *Journal de Gynécologie Obstétrique et Biologie de la Reproduction* 9: 741–749.

Nijhuis, H. G. J., H. J. Nordbeck, and S. J. M. Belleman. 1985. "Perinatale en zuigelingensterf in Amsterdam en Den Haag." *Tijdschrift voor Sociale Geneeskunde* 63: 409–414.

Peeters, R. F., and F. Van Der Veen. 1989. "De perinatale-en zuigelingensterfte van etnische minderheden in België/Vlaanderen." *Esoc* 18. Antwerp: University of Antwerp.

———. 1990. "De perinatale-en zuigelingensterfte van etnische minderheden in België/Vlaanderen." *Bevolking en Gezin* 1: 37–53.

Saurel-Cubizolles, M. J., Y. Rabarison, and C. Rumeau-Rouquette. 1984. "Études de groupes présentant des risques particuliers." In C. Rumeau-Rouquette, C. du Mazaubrun, and Y. Rabarison, eds., *Naître en France: 10 ans d'évolution.* Paris: Doin and INSERM, 149–159.

Saurel-Cubizolles, M. J., B. Stengel, M. Kaminski, and B. Blondel. 1986. "Surveillance prénatale et issue de la grossesse selon l'origine des femmes nées hors de France métropolitaine." *Journal de Gynécologie Obstétrique et Biologie de la Reproduction* 15: 19–27.

Siala Gaïgi, S., K. Jellouli, T. Doghri, and S. Gaïgi. 1990. "Alimentation de la femme enceinte et poids de l'enfant à la naissance." *La Tunisie Médicale* 68: 459–462.

Soltani, M. S., M. N. Guediche, A. Bchir, H. Ghanem, H. Pousse, and A. Braham. 1991. "Facteurs associés aux faibles poids de naissance dans le Sahel tunisien." *Archives Françaises de Pédiatrie* 48: 405–408.

Stengel, B., M. J. Saurel-Cubizolles, and M. Kaminski. 1986. "Pregnant Immigrant Women: Occupational Activity, Antenatal Care, and Outcome." *International Journal of Epidemiology* 15: 533–539.

Yudkin, P. L., S. Harlap, and M. Baras. 1983. "High Birthweight in an Ethnic Group of Low Socioeconomic Status." *British Journal of Obstetrics and Gynaecology* 90: 291–296.

5

How Do Flemish Health Providers Take Care of Their Turkish and Moroccan Patients?

Aimé De Muynck

Since the end of World War II, most West European countries have been confronted with massive immigration. In Belgium 9 percent of the population are immigrants, and Moroccans and Turks constitute 2.5 percent of the country's population. Migration is not a new phenomenon: emigration and immigration have always been a fundamental element of the demographic dynamics in Europe (Appleyaerd 1992). But there is a fundamental contextual difference between the earlier and present migrations to Belgium: since Social Security became available for everyone who is a resident or has a residential permit, the government is now responsible for the equitable distribution of health care services to legal immigrants as well as to indigenous citizens.

In the last few years, health care has been regionalized in Belgium, and responsibilities have been transferred to the Flemish, Walloon, and Brussels regional governments. In the Flemish region there reside now about 92,000 Turks and Moroccans (Poulain and Eggerickh 1990), which represents an important increase since 1988, when the official figure was 75,000 (Van de Mieroop, Peeters, and De Muynck 1989a). The increase is due to high fertility rates (Lesthaeghe and Surkyn 1994) and to the family reunion policy of our government, which allows immigration of spouses and other direct family members.

This article addresses the issue of the quality of care for Moroccan and Turkish migrants in the Flemish health care system. Specifically, it examines findings from a study of special health care provisions for migrants. Special provisions are tools to improve communication and ensure continuity of care and compliance with treatment regimens or preventive recommendations. They include posters, brochures, and video materials in the language of the target population, use of vocabulary lists, use of interpreters and/or immigrant personnel in reception areas, anamnesis and/or medical/paramedical activities, learning the language of the migrant, and becoming familiar with the culture of the most common immigrant groups.

Until 1983 Flemish research on migrants' health was descriptive and of limited value to policy makers. From 1984 to 1988 there were important methodological developments in various disciplines. During this period adapted measurement scales were developed, including an attitudinal scale for Turkish women (Timmerman, Claeys, and De Muynck 1989), an integration score (Ottenheim 1989), a holistic index for measurement of migrants' health (Schillemans et al. 1990), a hierarchical psychosomatic-complaints model for Turkish migrants (Gailly 1990), and a causal model for prenatal care for Turkish migrants (Da Silveira et al. 1988).

From 1989 on, there have been many surveys aimed at improving the quality of care for immigrants. Findings from the surveys indicate that migrant males consult physicians more frequently than females, and that immigrants' incidence of accidents and occupational diseases are much higher than that of Belgians and their sick leave days outnumber those of Belgians. Their perinatal mortality rates (Moroccans 14.4 per thousand, Turks 17.7 per thousand) are higher than that of Belgians (10.7 per thousand) (Buekens, Cleries Escayola, and Derom 1990), and the difference is not attributable to a lower birthweight or a higher prematurity rate of migrant babies. A comparative health survey (Peeters and Uniken Venema 1990) has shown that Turks in Antwerp, Belgium, do feel themselves healthier than Turks in Rotterdam, the Netherlands, although Turkish women in Antwerp complain more often of chronic health problems. The utilization of curative services, mainly consultations with general practitioners (De Muynck and Peeters 1994b) and the use of medicines (Verrept 1992), also presents ethnic differences.

Health behavior differs significantly between migrants and Belgians, and even between Moroccans and Turks, and also between Berbers and Arabic Moroccans (De Muynck 1993). On the average, migrants make less use of preventive services (Van der Stuyft et al. 1993), especially of primary and tertiary preventive care. Turkish and Moroccan pregnant women start consulting later in their pregnancy, consult less regularly, and practice fewer prenatal exercises than Belgians (De Muynck et al. 1993). Turks consult mainly public services, Moroccans mainly private practitioners (De Muynck 1993).

The level of knowledge and perceptions about diseases and health influence the use and assessment of health services. Belgians and Turkish migrants consider climate and natural causes as sources of ill health, while Moroccan migrants attribute illness to supernatural forces (Peeters 1986). Migrants view Western physicians positively and some allopathic medical values are easily incorporated into their own culture, while others are not. Turkish women prefer a two-children family and use family planning and even pregnancy interruption as a family planning strategy.

Theoretical Justification for Research on Special Provisions

During the last decade a number of initiatives were taken in Belgium to improve the health of ethnic minorities and to increase their accessibility to health services. Most initiatives are based on the assumption that the health care system is not sufficiently adapted to the needs and/or demands of ethnic minorities.

Many initiatives, mostly in the field of preventive care and health education (Koninklijk Commissariaat voor het Migrantenbeleid 1989), have been taken primarily by private general practitioners and by nongovernmental organizations (NGOs)—including the very interesting project of cultural brokerage by the Flemish Center of Ethnic Minorities and Health (De Ridder 1992, Verrept in this volume)—and are an expression of the attention given by the private health sector to immigrants. Special provisions are components of these initiatives and can be considered to be proxy indicators of the quality of care offered to migrants.

In Flanders there are no global indicators of migrants' accessibility to health services, although Schillemans et al.'s (1990) holistic index to measure patients' health status is a valuable first step. The Flemish government holds the view that migrants do not have special accessibility problems. In theory, this may be a correct position because every citizen has the right to use all existing health services, but in practice there are social, economic, cultural, and bureaucratic barriers to service utilization.

Health systems differ significantly in regard to special provisions for migrants (Bollini 1992); some national systems have developed provisions that can be defined as active, and so place the burden of improving accessibility and health services utilization on the system, while others tend to be passive, placing the burden on the users. Flanders's health system can be characterized as passive, a fact that was acknowledged by the Flemish minister of health in 1993 when he declared that the public health sector was in need of creating conditions to improve accessibility

Figure 5.1. Factors Influencing the Occurrence of
Special Provisions

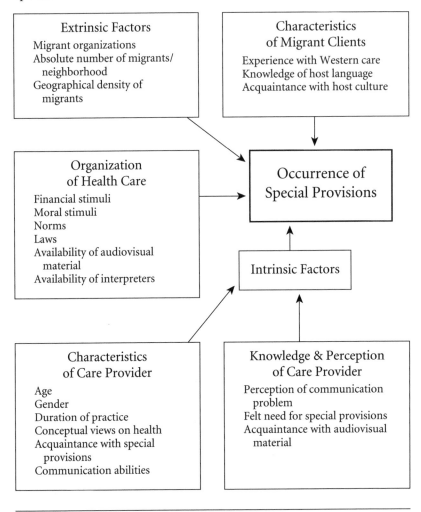

for migrants as well as of hiring migrant staff. On the other hand, Italian
and French health systems, with their special services for migrants, and
the Swedish system, which routinely offers interpreter's services, can be
considered to be active. Health systems with active provisions tend to op-
timize the adaptation of migrants to the host society (Bahl 1993, Berry
1992); consequently, it is more likely that in these countries migrants,
both at the individual and collective level, enjoy better health conditions.

DETERMINANTS OF SPECIAL PROVISIONS

What factors determine that a health care provider makes special provisions in order to improve his or her communication with and the quality of care for his or her migrant clients? With a better understanding of the determinants, it would be easier for health authorities to stimulate care providers to use (more) special provisions. Insights into the determinants and their causal pathway could function as a driving force to fill gaps in our health care systems.

Figure 5.1 presents the main factors that determine the use of special provisions. It distinguishes between extrinsic and intrinsic factors. Extrinsic factors, such as the residential density of migrants, refer to potential determinants outside the direct domain of the health provider. Intrinsic factors, such as the age of the care provider, refer to the awareness existing inside the health care system of special provisions. As will be discussed later, our study attempts to take into account intrinsic as well as extrinsic factors.

UNIVERSALISTIC VERSUS PARTICULARISTIC SCOPE

In theory, all legal residents have access to Flemish health care services. With the exception of those with special medical problems—often related to specific age groups—every citizen, regardless of ethnic origin, can consult any care provider at any time. Migrants are welcome at all levels of care, and until now no special services exclusively for migrants have been organized. This policy can be considered to be universalistic and, in theory, is very equitable: the government organizes and finances services for the entire population, and the services are the same for all citizens.

We need to examine how the universalistic policy functions in practice. At present, in spite of the fact that a series of isolated initiatives have been taken and have been proven to contribute significantly to better care, there is no evidence that the Flemish health system has given sufficient attention to migrants. For example, male and—to an even greater degree—female Moroccan and Turkish patients experience major communication problems with health providers (Putsch 1985). According to Spruit (1986), communication with Moroccan and Turkish clients is problematic for general practitioners and pharmacists.

Many care providers are mistakenly convinced that they can communicate perfectly well with their immigrant patients (Ferrant 1989). Communication between physicians and migrants presents many difficulties:

for example, according to one study, only one in four Turkish patients understand the whole explanation given during a medical visit to a general practitioner (Eylenbosch and Peeters 1984). Communication problems between health care providers and clients are a manifestation of a general communication problem between migrants and natives. Thus, studies in the Netherlands (Voorham 1988) have found that 60 percent of migrants feel that they are not well understood by the Dutch people. Turks experience communication difficulties more often than Moroccans, and there is an obvious link between communication problems and language proficiency. About 38 percent experience a major communication problem several times per week, and this occurs more frequently among women than among men. Even more striking is the fact that 21 percent of Moroccan women never experience communication problems with local Dutch people because they do not have any contacts with them.

Both health care providers and clients influence the communication process. On the part of the provider, factors that determine the quality of the communication include understanding of the language and culture of the patient, attitudes toward migrants, and communication skills. On the part of the migrant, the factors are host-country language proficiency, knowledge of the culture of the receiving country, and expectations toward the health services.

Language is a major obstacle to communication. "The greater the need for oral communication, the greater the communication problems," states Voorham (1988). The language barrier is associated with the "enclosure" of first-generation immigrant women; their isolation has a negative impact on the verbalization of their health care needs. The language barrier makes it difficult to establish a relationship of mutual trust between provider and client, to get a full medical history, to make a correct diagnosis, to follow the treatment schedule correctly, and to have a correct understanding of the patient's psychosocial background.

Linguistic barriers can be overcome through interpreters. However, until now there has been little use of interpreters in the Netherlands and even less in Belgium. Family members or friends are often asked to translate, but for a number of reasons this solution is far from adequate. Only occasionally is special educational material used to overcome the language barrier. Communication problems can also be caused by negative attitudes of care providers toward ethnic minorities and by their lack of communication skills. Cultural barriers also need to be overcome. Migrants assess their well-being and health conditions from the point of view of their own cultural background, which frequently is unknown to the health care provider.

Communication difficulties can result in late or inappropriate diagnosis, underreporting of medical problems, faulty therapeutic decisions by the medical staff, insufficient communication of explanatory models to the immigrant, a prolonged atmosphere of uncertainty concerning diagnosis and prescribed treatment, incorrect interpretation of medical prescriptions, physician shopping by patients, lack of compliance with medical regimens, less equitable medical care, a hostile social climate, and increasing racism.

The Research on Special Provisions

The objective of this study was to get a better understanding of the use of special provisions in relation to geographical area and type of care provider and to recommend appropriate measures to improve health care delivery to Moroccans and Turks in the Flemish region. The study carried out in 1988–90 identified all municipalities with at least one hundred Moroccan or Turkish residents. There are sixty such municipalities in Flanders, where 95.3 percent of all Turkish or Moroccan immigrants in Flanders reside. Within each of the sixty municipalities we identified all individuals and services offering health care. We included the following health care providers and services:

- At the primary health care level: general practitioners, pharmacists, public welfare centers, child and family welfare services, individuals or services concerned with home care, psychological welfare services, regional branches of medical insurance organizations, and outpatient clinics
- At the secondary level: specialists, physiotherapists, and psycho-medical-social (PMS) centers
- At the tertiary level: hospitals
- At the fourth level: psychiatric hospitals, special care institutions for children, and centers for the mentally handicapped

Data gathering was similar in all municipalities. In each of the sixty municipalities, all care providers were interviewed by phone regarding the presence of migrant clients and the use of special provisions. After a pilot study in Antwerp (Van de Mieroop, Peeters, and De Muynck 1989b), the research was extended to the rest of Flanders.

FREQUENCY OF SPECIAL PROVISIONS

Contacts between migrants and care providers were quite frequent: about 42 percent of providers regularly saw migrants, and 29 percent of those who did see migrants made special provisions. Special provisions were used at each of the four levels of care, but there were significant differences by levels in the frequency and in the number of provisions (see table 5.1). The lowest percentage was at the secondary level, the primary level scored somewhat higher, and the third and fourth levels scored considerably higher.

At each level we observed considerable differences according to the type of care provided, the type of institution, and the density of the migrant population. The curative sector used fewer special provisions than the preventive one. Within the former, special provisions were introduced by providers working in the diagnostic sector more frequently than in technical areas; for example, orthopedic specialists used special provisions significantly more often than physiotherapists (De Muynck and Peeters 1994a) and pediatricians and internists used them more frequently than surgeons (Peeters and De Muynck 1994).

Providers working with Moroccan and Turkish clients used leaflets (13 percent), persons familiar with the language and culture of the clients (9 percent), nonprofessional interpreters (8 percent) and interpreting centers (2 percent), vocabulary lists (4 percent), and other kinds of special provisions (4 percent). Primary- and secondary-level providers used mainly leaflets and persons familiar with the language and culture of patients, while third- and fourth-level providers used interpreters (see table 5.2).

We also conducted in 1990–91 a study of a representative sample of 201 general practitioners who had Moroccan and Turkish patients. They were regularly confronted with some fifteen major complaints or problems by their migrant clients. The top five of these (by percentage) consisted of medical problems (in descending order: gastrointestinal disorders, asthma and respiratory disorders, gynecological and obstetric problems, cardiovascular disorders, and accidents), while psycho-socio-administrative and welfare problems were seen less frequently.

Our study of what general practitioners do when confronted with one of these fifteen problems or disorders showed that their attitudes were not determined by whether or not they made special provisions. This was a most unexpected result. We had expected general practitioners with special provisions to have a more global approach toward their migrant

Table 5.1. Care-Providing Institutions with Immigrant Clients
and Special Provisions

Care Institutions	Total Number of Institutions (column 1)	Institutions Serving Immigrants (column 2)	Institutions w/ Special Provisions (column 3)	Percentage of Institutions w/ Special Provisions (column 3 : 2)
General practitioners	1,753	724	209	29
Pharmacists	947	538	92	17
OCMW local centers[a]	86	55	30	55
Kind en Gezin Clinics[b]	356	184	112	61
Home care	134	69	25	36
Psychological health centers	92	27	14	52
Regional health-insurance offices	114	63	27	43
Outpatient clinics	40	23	12	52
Physiotherapists	1,224	237	21	9
Specialists	1,313	615	125	20
PMS centers	112	89	62	70
Hospitals	114	97	46	47
Child special-care institutions	202	61	28	46
Institutions for the handicapped	201	46	24	52
Psychiatric hospitals	38	16	9	56
Total	6,726	2,884	836	29

a. Welfare Center of the Villages.
b. Clinics run by the National Mother and Child Care Organization, called Child and
  Family Clinics since 1980.

patients than general practitioners without special provisions. Many general practitioners, including those who did not take special provisions, expressed their desire to approach those specific problems in a more holistic way. This was especially the case for problems due to lack of integration in the host society, psychosocial problems of migrant females,

Table 5.2. Type and Occurrence of Special Provisions per
Level of Care

Type	Level				P-Values
	Primary (%)	Secondary (%)	Third (%)	Fourth (%)	
Leaflets	16	9	11	4	10^{-8}
Auxiliary personnel	10	8	11	5	.11
Interpreters	6	7	26	24	10^{-10}
Interpreting centers	2	.5	5	14	10^{-7}
Other	2	4	8	15	10^{-8}

Note: P-values have been calculated through X^2 tests.

and alcohol and drug abuse. General practitioners were generally pleased with their handling of somatic problems such as heart diseases, gastrointestinal disorders, genitourinary disorders, and accidents in their migrant patients.

The wish of general practitioners to make (more) special provisions was found to be correlated with their wish for a more holistic approach to migrants' complaints, the size of the migrant clientele (the larger the number of migrant clients the more they considered special provisions to be necessary), the experienced problems with the culture and/or language of the migrant clients, and the age of the general practitioner (the younger their ages, the more they considered special provisions to be necessary).

Discussion

How much attention does the Flemish health care system give to Moroccan and Turkish migrants? The review of the literature suggests that the health status of migrants is lower than that of natives and that migrants less adequately use preventive and curative services. It would be logical to conclude that health care providers should pay more attention to migrants, but research indicates that in fact they pay less attention to them. The Flemish health system does not require the use of special provisions and does not provide a financial compensation to those who use them. It is not surprising that only 29 percent of providers with migrant clients use them. The Flemish policy toward migrants can be best characterized as passive: let each provider solve his or her own communication problems. The special provisions themselves are passive: they consist of brochures and leaflets, while active provisions such as interpreters, videos, and auxiliary staff acquainted with the language and culture of the migrants are the exception. As a result, the health system places an undue responsibility on the migrants themselves.

As indicated, special provisions are used differently by the various health care levels. It is unfortunate that only a relatively small number of primary-level providers use special provisions, because they are the first point of contact with the health care system. Even the number of general practitioners who use special provisions is not very high. Yet it is at this level that personal support, integral care, and continuity should be provided.

The utilization of special provisions by general practitioners, pharmacists, specialists, child and family welfare centers, and home care centers is positively correlated with the number of migrants in the community. The higher the percentage of migrants, the higher the use of special provisions. Even a slight increase in the percentage could cause an increase in the number of institutions using provisions (De Muynck and Peeters 1992, Peeters et al. 1992). An exception to this rule are the physiotherapists (De Muynck and Peeters 1992). Why this is the case is a perplexing question because Mediterranean immigrants have a high prevalence of osteomuscular problems (Van Wieringen et al. 1987). A possible interpretation could be that physiotherapists, as a professional group, do not take into account the role that culture has in the somatization of psychosocial problems, and thus fail to appreciate their potential role in the diagnosis and treatment of psychosomatic problems of migrants. Additional research is needed to understand how population density induces practitioners to use special provisions.

The organization of care also influences the usage of special provisions. Practitioners working in group practice tend to use provisions more frequently than those in solo practice. The former are generally organized by regional authorities whose policies frequently, but not always, encourage special provisions.

As indicated, different levels of care utilize different types of special provisions. It is unfortunate that primary- and secondary-level providers make little use of interpreters who translate words and concepts and, by doing so, could be very instrumental in facilitating a holistic approach to care (Ferrant 1988) and in improving problem recognition.

How do care providers assess the value of the special provisions at their disposal? It has been mentioned that the presence of special provisions does not seem to influence greatly the way health providers practice health care. To us this is an indication that perhaps special provisions are not the best indicators of quality of care for migrant clients, particularly when the provisions are of the passive type. Passive provisions have a limited potential to improve provider-client relations. Another surprising finding was that once care providers use special provisions, they feel the need to improve their scope. Age and exposure to cultural and/or linguistic problems are variables that also influence the practitioner's need to use special provisions.

Our study was not designed to assess the impact of special provisions on the quality of care offered to migrants. Nevertheless, it is our opinion that they facilitate contact between care providers and their migrant patients, improve trust in the physician (Schillemans and Zeineb 1979), strengthen the continuity of preventive and curative care, promote a global approach to the problems of health and welfare encountered by ethnic minorities, help to empower the people who usually have least access to the Flemish health system—in particular migrant women, who are the most powerless (De Ridder 1988)—and make health services culturally more accessible and consequently more equitable (Whitehead 1992).

Our findings suggest that migrant health care policies should include, but not be limited to, special provisions. Other essential elements of migrant health policies are the elimination of ethnic discrimination, availability of reliable information on health conditions and health behavior of migrants, participation of migrants in decision making, and minority recruitment into the health system (Bahl 1993).

Acknowledgments

The fieldwork for this study was made possible by a grant from the Belgian Fund for Medical Scientific Research. We thank the members of the steering group and especially the late Professor Dr. R. Peeters for their support and guidance.

References

Appleyaerd, R. T. 1992. "Immigration and Development: A Global Agenda for the Future." *International Migration Review* 30: 17–31.

Bahl, V. 1993. "The Development of a Black and Ethnic Minority Health Policy at the Department of Health." *Innovation, Migration, and Health* 6: 67–74.

Berry, J. W. 1992. "Acculturation and Adaptation in a New Society." *International Migration Review* 30: 69–85.

Buekens, P., M. Cleries Escayola, and R. Derom. 1990. "Perinatal Outcomes of Immigrants in Belgium." *Archives of Public Health* 48: 33–40.

Bollini, P. 1992. "Health Policies for Immigrant Populations in the 1990s: A Comparative Study in Seven Receiving Countries." *International Migration Review* 30: 103–119.

Da Silveira V., A. De Muynck, C. Timmerman, and P. Van der Stuyft. 1988. "Development and Uses of a Conceptual Model in the Study of Antenatal Services Utilization by Migrant Women in Belgium." Working paper no. 19. Antwerp: Department of Community Health, Institute of Tropical Medicine, Antwerp.

De Muynck, A. 1993. ["Care Demand and Supply for Migrant Patients in the Flemish Region."] Doctoral diss., University of Antwerp.

De Muynck, A., M. Lammers, A. Van Hoof, and L. Schillemans. 1993. "Rol van de interactie hulpverlener-patiënte." *HUISARTS NU* 22: 60–62, 67.

De Muynck, A., and R. Peeters. 1992. ["Which Special Provisions Are Taken by the Health Care System for Ali and Fatima in Flanders? Empirical Research Results."] *Esoc* 30. Antwerp: University of Antwerp.

———. 1994a. ["Do Our Physiotherapists Take Special Provisions for Ali and Fatima?"] *KINE 2000* 5: 13–15.

———. 1994b. ["How Healthy are Ali and Fatima?"] *Esoc* 30. Antwerp: University of Antwerp.

De Ridder, R. 1988. ["Family Practitioners for Turkish Migrants."] In B. Alis-Verisi, ed., [*Care and Health Promotion for Turkish Migrants*]. Brussels: Koning Boudewijnstichting, pp. 133–139.

De Ridder, R. 1992. "Intercultural Brokerage in Heath Care: A Project in Flanders." *Medische Antropologie* 4: 179–183.

Eylenbosch, W., and R. Peeters. 1984. ["Illness and Health of Moroccan Immigrants at Hoboken, Antwerp."] Unpublished report. University of Antwerp.

Ferrant, L. 1988. ["Communication."] *Bijblijven* 4: 33–39.

Ferrant, L. 1989. ["Communication and Culture."] *HUISARTS NU* 18: 493–496.

Gailly A. 1990. "Etnogeneeskunde en Psychosomiatische Klachten bij Turken." *Acta Medica Catholica* 59: 19–28.

Koninklijk Commissariaat voor het Migrantenbeleid. 1989. ["Integration Policy Making: A Task of Long Duration. Part 1: Norms and Preliminary Propositions; Part 3: Facts and Final Propositions."] Brussels.

Lesthaeghe, R., and J. Surkyn. 1994. ["Turkish and Moroccan Women in Belgium: Family Creation and Values in Generation Changes."] *Bevolking en Gezin.* Brussels: Flemish Ministry of Health, pp. 9–51.

Ottenheim C. 1989. "De Gezondheidsspecifieke beheersingsorientatie: Een

Vergelijkend Onderzoek bij Turken en Belgen in Antwerpen." Doctoral diss., University of Limburg, Maastricht.

Peeters, R. 1986. "Health and Illness of Moroccan Immigrants in the City of Antwerp, Belgium." *Social Science and Medicine* 22: 679–685.

Peeters, R., and A. De Muynck. 1994. ["Which Special Provisions Do Specialists Take for Ali and Fatima?"] *Tijdschrift Geneeskunde* 50: 399–406.

Peeters, R., A. Segaert, E. Van de Mieroop, and A. De Muynck. 1992. ["What Care Does the Flemish Health Care System Offer to Ali and Fatima?"] *Esoc* 25. Antwerp: University of Antwerp.

Peeters, R., and P. Uniken Venema. 1990. ["Coping with Illness: A Comparative Research of Curative Consumption of Turkish Minorities in Rotterdam and Antwerp."] *Archives of Public Health* 48: 41–57.

Poulain, M., and T. Eggerickh. 1990. ["Demographic Characteristics of the Foreign Population in Belgian Cities, 1983–1988."] *Bevolking en Gezin* 1: 77–92.

Putsch, R. W. 1985. "Cross-cultural Communication: The Special Care of Interpreters in Health Care." *Journal of the American Medical Association* 254: 3344–3348.

Schillemans, L., A. De Muynck, P. Van der Stuyft, R. Saenen, and R. Baeten. 1990. "Assessment of Patients' Health Status in Family Medicine." *Quality Assurance in Health Care* 2: 161–170.

Schillemans, L., and T. Zeineb. 1979. ["Health Care for Foreigners: Challenge and Test Criterion."] *Metamedica* 58: 3–9.

Spruit, I. P. 1986. "Health Care for Labour Migrants: Perception of Problems." In C. Colledge, H. A. Van Geuns, and P. G. Svensson, eds., *Migration and Health*. WHO-Europe, ICP/SPM 050(3): pp. 32–75.

Timmerman C., W. Claeys, and A. De Muynck. 1989. "Denken over Waarden: Attitudes van Turkse Migrantenvrouwen Tegenover een Westers Waardensysteem." *Cultuur en Migratie*. Brussels.

Van de Mieroop, E., R. Peeters, and A. De Muynck. 1989a. "Atlas of Ethnic Minorities: Geographical Distribution of Moroccans and Turks in Flanders and Brussels." Antwerp: Institute of Tropical Medicine and University of Antwerp.

———. 1989b. ["Special Provisions Taken by the Antwerp Family Practitioner."] *HUISARTS NU* 18: 517–519.

Van der Stuyft, P., M. Woodward, J. Armstrong, and A. De Muynck. 1993. "Uptake of Preventive Health Care among Mediterranean Migrants in Belgium." *Journal of Epidemiology and Community Health* 47: 10–13.

Van Wieringen, J. C. M., A. Leentvaar-Kuypers, H. J. Brouwer, A. C. Slegt, and H. A. Van Kassel-Al. 1987. ["Morbidity Profile and Medical Actions with Ethnic Groups."] *Tijdschrift Sociale Gezondheidzorg* 65: 587–592.

Verrept, H. 1992. "Moroccan Migrants and Their Medicines." *Medische Anthropologie* 4: 184–198.

Voorham, A. J. J. 1988. ["Communication Problems with Migrants: An Empirical Research of Felt Communication Problems of Turkish and Moroccan Clients of the Juvenile Health Care System in Rotterdam."] *Gemeentelyke Geneeskundige en Gezondheidsdienst, afdeling Gezondheidsvoorlichting en Opvoeding, Rotterdam* 86: 116–142.

Whitehead, M. 1992. "The Concepts and Principles of Equity and Health." *International Journal of Health Services* 22: 429–445.

6

Health Advocates in Belgian Health Care

Hans Verrept and Fred Louckx

This article reports on a health advocacy program for Moroccan and Turkish patients in Flanders and Brussels (Belgium). The program was introduced in 1991 as an initiative of the Center for Health and Ethnic Minorities (CEMG), an interdisciplinary group of researchers and practitioners with expertise in the field of ethnic minorities and health. The program has been funded as an experiment for a period of five years by several Flemish and Brussels ministries.

About sixty Moroccan and Turkish women were recruited and trained as health advocates and started working in various sectors of Belgian health care (mainly in mother and baby health care, in hospitals, and in preventive medicine for schoolchildren). The aim of the health advocacy program is to improve the quality of health care delivered to Moroccan and Turkish patients. This should ultimately lead to an improvement of the relatively unfavorable health status of these ethnic minorities. Although large-scale health status surveys have been carried out in neither the Moroccan nor the Turkish communities in Belgium, it is generally assumed by researchers, practitioners, and policy makers that the health status of these minorities is lower than that of the indigenous Belgian population. Findings from small-scale health surveys carried out in Belgium lend support to this assumption, as do findings of similar research in other European countries (Peeters and De Muynck 1994, Ahmad 1992).

Research of De Muynck (1990) has made clear that Moroccan and Turkish patients face major problems when they make use of Belgian health care services. The language and culture barriers, combined with the fact that little or no special measures have been taken to adapt the health care system to the presence of large numbers of relatively recent immigrants, seriously hamper the effective and smooth delivery of health care services to these patients, as has been observed in other countries (Saldov and Chow 1994). This leads to a situation in which ethnic minority patients may systematically receive lower-quality health care than indigenous patients.

The intervention of the health advocates is expected to contribute to the quality of care for this population, mainly through the improvement of the communication between health professionals and ethnic minority patients. The health advocates are to play four roles, which are the roles that have been described by Kaufert and Koolage (1984): (1) the health advocates act as interpreters, (2) they provide information to health professionals about linguistic and cultural factors that may affect patients' behavior and the process and outcome of the health care intervention, (3) they provide information to patients about various aspects of "biomedical culture" (explaining biomedical concepts and the functioning of health care institutions, providing patient education, and obtaining meaningful informed consent), and (4) they are advocates for the ethnic minority patients (this involves speaking on behalf of the patients and defending their best interests and legitimate consumer's demands). This last role may entail opposing health professionals' views.

In 1992 the Department of Medical-Social Sciences of the VUB (Free University of Brussels) was asked by one of the funding ministries to carry out an evaluation study of the effects of the health advocacy program. The study described below attempts to answer two questions:

1. Does working with health advocates lead to an improvement of the quality of health care delivered to ethnic minority patients (in the Belgian project)?
2. Which problems are associated with the introduction of health advocates and might in this way reduce the effectiveness of the health advocacy program?

Research Design

As empirical research on the effects of health advocates on the quality of care is scarce, we decided early on in the project to opt for a qualitative and exploratory research design (Rocheron, Dickinson, and Khan 1988). A central problem of our research was to decide on the criteria to be used to judge the evolution of the quality of care. It is relatively easy to develop precise standards or criteria for the evaluation of very specific and technical aspects of health care. In our research, however, we were confronted with the task of judging the evolution of the quality of care under the influence of the health advocacy program in a wide variety of health care settings. The fact that in most of the domains where the health advocates are working no explicit evaluation criteria or standards were available added to this problem. It soon became clear to us that it would be unrealistic to try to develop consensus texts (containing explicit standards or criteria to be used to judge the evolution of the quality of care) with the large and very heterogeneous group of health professionals involved in the health advocacy program. We therefore decided to make use of the implicit criteria of the health professionals (made explicit during the interviews) as one of the ways to get information on the evolution of the quality of care.

In all, twenty-eight in-depth interviews were conducted with health professionals who had experience in working with Moroccan health advocates in mother and baby care and/or hospitals.[1] Eight medical doctors and nine social nurses working for mother and baby health care centers were interviewed. Of the eleven health professionals working in the hospitals, seven are either social workers or social nurses, three are nurses, and one is a pediatrician. The number of health professionals was judged to be adequate as no new information was forthcoming from the last health professionals who joined the study. The large number of social workers and social nurses in our hospital sample is indicative of the fact that other categories of health professionals do not very often make use of the services of the health advocates. The in-depth interviews were designed to collect data on (1) the frequency of the cooperation of the health professionals with the health advocates, (2) the tasks performed by the health advocates, (3) the effects on the quality of care (both at the level of process and outcome of care and at the level of perceived patient satisfaction), and (4) the problems associated with the introduction of the health advocacy program.

To get a more complete picture of the functioning of the health advocacy program, we also conducted in-depth interviews with twenty-one experienced Moroccan health advocates. As members of the target group of the program, they were in an excellent position to develop an awareness of the problems experienced by ethnic minority patients in health care and especially to see whether the program was able to resolve these problems. In addition, health advocates were specifically asked to recount "compliments and complaints" they had received from clients about the introduction of the health advocacy program. We also asked them whether they were aware of certain constraints (e.g., the health advocates' lack of medical knowledge, or unwillingness on the part of health professionals) that were hampering the effectiveness of the program and how these could be overcome.

Finally, thirty-one randomly selected clients of the Moroccan advocates (twenty from the mother and baby health care services and eleven from the hospitals) were interviewed. The aim of these semistructured interviews was to collect further information on the effects of the health advocacy program on some aspects of patient satisfaction. In particular, we wanted to check whether the introduction of the program met some resistance by patients, which might affect their willingness to make use of the services involved. Interviews with the clients of the health advocates were also conducted to get a complementary view of the activities performed by the health advocates.

Interviews with health professionals and health advocates usually lasted between forty-five and ninety minutes, and those with health advocates' clients mostly between thirty and sixty minutes. Interviews with health professionals and health advocates were conducted by the researcher. Most clients were interviewed by a Moroccan or an Algerian female interviewer to avoid information biases as a result of the sex and ethnicity of the researcher (Andersen 1993). All interview materials (with the exception of the client interviews, which were not tape-recorded) were transcribed and analyzed with Textbase Alpha, a computer program for qualitative data analysis. Data obtained from the interviews with health professionals, health advocates, and clients were then compared to check the reliability of the interview material.

Results

INFORMANTS' CHARACTERISTICS

Comparison of social and demographic characteristics of the health advocates and their clients shows that both groups are linguistically and culturally very close to each other. Most health advocates are second-generation immigrants whose parents came to Belgium in the 1960s or early 1970s. Their parents, like most Moroccan immigrants in Belgium, emigrated from the northern regions of Morocco (especially the Rif and the large Moroccan cities in the north such as Tétouan, Oujda, and Tanger). Fourteen of the twenty-one Moroccan health advocates consider themselves to be ethnically Berber and have Dhamazight, a Berber language, as their mother tongue. Most Berber health advocates are also fluent in Moroccan Arabic. The other health advocates consider themselves to be ethnically Arab. Their mother tongue is Moroccan Arabic, none speaking Dhamazight. The presence of a large number of Berbers among the health advocates is important because the largest proportion of the Moroccan community in Belgium is of Berber descent and because a relatively large group of first-generation Berber women have only very limited or absolutely no linguistic skills in either Moroccan Arabic, French, or Dutch (Hermans 1991a). Most health advocates had a low educational status when they joined the program, which again is characteristic of most Moroccan women in Belgium.

A striking point of difference between the health advocates and most second-generation Moroccan women in Belgium is the high proportion of health advocates who live in situations felt to be undesirable and possibly even dishonorable by a relatively large section of the Moroccan community in Belgium: four live alone, two live with a friend without being married, and four live with or are married to a Belgian partner. These living arrangements may increase health advocates' vulnerability to gossip in the closely knit communities in which they are living and working (Renaerts 1991). They are also indicative of the different views many of these health advocates hold on the role and position of women in society and may, of course, apart from economic necessity, have played a major role in their decision to start working. The fact that health advocates are linguistically and culturally close to the population they serve is considered by some authors to be an important prerequisite for the smooth functioning of health advocacy programs (Anderson 1986). The success of such programs may be seriously hampered by health advocates' insufficient skills in the language of their clients and by an inability to provide accurate information to the health professionals about cultural issues that are relevant to the delivery of health care.

The study sample of the Moroccan health advocates' clients consisted of twenty young women who went to the mother and baby health care centers. Half of them are first-generation immigrants, the other half are immigrants of the second generation. Thirteen of them have no or very little knowledge of either Dutch or French and are completely dependent on health advocates or informal interpreters for their communication with health professionals. Of the eleven hospital patients (five males, six females), eight are of the first generation. Only three of them have absolutely no knowledge of French or Dutch. The three second-generation patients all are fluent in either French or Dutch. The fact that the patients in the hospital sample have a better command of Dutch or French is probably related to the presence of men in this group.

Of the seventeen health professionals at the mother and baby health care centers, only two are men. Most of them have been working with a health advocate for at least half a day every week for a period of more than a year. This means that they have ample experience in cooperating with a health advocate. This is not the case for the eleven health professionals in the hospitals. Four of them had relatively little experience (less than five interventions) in working with a health advocate. The problems faced by the researchers in finding health professionals with a fair amount of experience in working with a health advocate are indicative of the problems associated with the introduction of health advocates in the hospitals.

EFFECTS ON THE QUALITY OF CARE

The three groups of informants confirm that the introduction of health advocates leads to an important increase in the quality of care, if adequate use is made of their services. All of the health professionals state that the health advocacy program should be continued and should become a regular service available to ethnic minority patients and health staff.

Most important of all the improvements is the fact that health advocates facilitate the exchange of correct and detailed information between health staff and patients. This is a consequence not only of the presence of an interpreter but also of the fact that patients are less inhibited about telling their stories in the presence of the health advocate (and/or in the absence of an informal interpreter). In addition, our data suggest that adaptations at the level of communication strategies and style contribute to the effectiveness of communication with Moroccan patients. These improvements have far-reaching effects, as we will illustrate with quotations from our interview material presented below.

Improved Communication. Health professionals point out that the program increases their ability to diagnose certain conditions and to differentiate between them (e.g., finding clues as to whether continuing feelings of discomfort are related to somatic or psychosocial problems). Taking a detailed anamnesis (in the way it is taken from indigenous patients) has become possible with some Moroccan patients only since the introduction of the health advocate. An example of the described improvements is given in this passage from an interview with a social nurse working in a mother and baby health care center:

I don't think that I am doing my work as thoroughly without the health advocate. Sometimes I have to make a first home visit without her. Without her, I am working much faster; I am not going into things as much. They [the clients] are giving short answers, and I am asking short questions, using simple language. I believe that the health advocate is necessary, because it turns our home visits into meaningful experiences for the clients and for us. We understand them, they understand us. They can ask questions—they often want to ask many questions—but then there is the language barrier. . . . Without the health advocate, you leave the patients with the uneasy feeling that you haven't been able to do much for them.

A general practitioner, also involved in the program at a mother and baby health care center, gives another example of the effects of the improved—be it indirect—communication with clients:

One of my Moroccan patients has very heavy children. . . . She would certainly not have had the courage to tell me how she is feeding her babies. But she did tell the health advocate, during one of the home visits. So now I know. It is important to me to know that the excessive weight of the babies is simply a consequence of eating too much, and that I don't have to start looking for a metabolical disorder.

Health professionals and patients alike point out that the interventions of the health advocates make smoother health care delivery possible because, as a result of the improved communication, they can now cooperate better. This is well illustrated in the following quote from a health advocate working at a hospital:

A first attempt [without the assistance of the health advocate] to perform a gastroscopy on a fifty-seven-year-old Berberian woman had to be aborted because the patient got into a state of panic. Talking to the woman, I found out she had thought she was undergoing surgery. The second attempt to do the gastroscopy was successful. I translated the doctor's instructions. He was surprised it was so unproblematic this time, and that the patient cooperated so well.

In addition, we find systematic evidence that many Moroccan patients find it easier to talk to the health advocate about a whole range of topics than to Belgian health professionals. Our data suggest that this is also the case for some second-generation Moroccans whose Dutch or French is in many cases better than their Moroccan Arabic or Dhamazight. According to these patients, the health advocates are able to understand certain messages better because "things are different in the Moroccan community and the health advocates know what they are like." Health professionals point out that many problems, especially in the domains of family relationships, marital problems, and contraception, were not easily discussed before the health advocates started working and consequently often remained hidden from them. Some Moroccan patients even try to create a positive image of their family life and their social position to fight the negative prejudices of Belgian health professionals. We found a relatively large number of cases in which Moroccan patients at first presented a completely different image of their psychosocial situation than they did later on in the presence of the health advocate. In some cases, these revelations had far-reaching effects on the strategy to be followed by the health professionals. For example, a health advocate working at a hospital said:

> An older Moroccan woman had always claimed that she was well cared for and even financially supported by her son, who in reality turned out to be a drug addict and a thief, stealing whatever he could lay his hands on from his destitute mother. Following the revelations made to the health advocate, a meeting with the son was organized. The social worker of the hospital found out the son could claim a social security benefit, which was arranged for. This intervention considerably reduced the stress associated with the financial problems of the family.

Health advocates and their clients tell us that clients are supported and encouraged to ask questions of health professionals when they are hesitating to do so. Clients sometimes think that asking all their questions might be too much of a burden to the health professionals or that their questions might be considered ridiculous (e.g., questions about bed-wetting). Health professionals state that many questions were not asked before, either because of the language barrier or because of patients' inhibitions. Some patients report that certain topics could not be discussed with health professionals in the past because discussing them in the presence of the informal interpreter would have embarrassed both patient and interpreter. For example, a forty-seven-year-old Berberian man said:

> I used to be my wife's interpreter when she went to see the gynecologist, and when she delivered. To avoid feelings of shame, I stood a little apart from my wife. It is better that there are health advocates available now, because it is better to discuss women's affairs between women. There are things I cannot say to my wife, even if I am her husband.

Folk illnesses, such as possession by spirits (*jnun*), and traditional remedies, such as consulting a Koranic teacher (*fqih*), are also more readily discussed with the health advocate, as are emotions and mental states. This may seriously affect the process and outcome of the health care intervention. It has been observed that Moroccan patients often make use of traditional remedies and consult traditional healers (Hermans 1991b). In a number of cases, patients had planned to stop the biomedical treatment and to rely only on the therapeutic skills of a traditional healer. A health advocate working at a hospital explained:

A patient underwent dialysis, and intended to travel to Morocco to a spa [Sidi Harazem] and to go on a pilgrimage, without telling the health professionals anything about her plans. She would not have been dialyzed in Morocco, if she had not told me about her plans. Together with the health professional, I was able to convince her of the necessity of the dialytic treatment, also in Morocco. A Moroccan dialysis center was contacted, and the woman was regularly dialyzed during her stay at Sidi Harazem.

Health professionals point out that this patient might not be alive today if she had not been dialyzed during her stay in Morocco, a situation they had witnessed with other patients before the health advocacy program was introduced. Patients' readiness to reveal their mental states to the health advocate made it possible to meet their need for psychological support. Providing such support is an important task of the mother and baby health care centers. Making psychological support also available for Moroccan patients is seen as one of the major benefits of the program. A considerable number of the young mothers have only recently arrived in Belgium (the so-called imported brides), feel cut off from their friends and family, and are leading isolated lives in a country with which they are not familiar. A social nurse working for a mother and baby health care center said:

I have to admit that we did not give psychological support to Moroccan mothers before, because they were unable to express their emotions. It is very beneficial for them now to have someone who can lend them an ear. Because many of them are very lonely. During our home visits, they now get an opportunity to pour out their heart. It is very important that we can now break through their isolation.

Patients' assumption that health advocates will understand their problems better is not the only reason they are more willing to talk about certain subjects with them. Health advocates describe how they adapt questions to the communication style of Moroccan patients. They point out that the way Belgian health care practitioners ask many questions is counterproductive and leads to an unwillingness on the part of the patients to discuss their problems. Health advocates ask more personal questions in an indirect, evocative way. This strategy, illustrated below, makes it clear to the patient that the health professional would like to discuss a certain topic. Still, it remains possible for the patient not to discuss the theme, without having to be rude. This technique has been recommended by Eppink, a Dutch specialist in cross-cultural communication, to get more personal information from Mediterranean patients (Eppink 1981). An example of this technique was given by a health advocate working for a mother and baby health care center:

> Some health care practitioners ask: Have you got problems? I never do that. If you ask a question like that, they [the patients] say: What problems, I haven't got any problems. I say: You're looking tired, haven't you slept well, has the baby kept you awake? If they want to talk about their problems, they will do it then.

Health advocates also report that they use specific communication strategies to correct their clients' misconceptions and to convince them of the importance of taking their medication regularly, for example. Evidence from our data suggests that health advocates are much more effective in convincing patients to undergo surgery, to stick to certain therapeutic regimens, and to consult specialists or paramedics (for example, physiotherapists, a group of health professionals that is unknown to a large section of the Belgian Moroccan community). Many health care practitioners recount interventions of health advocates with considerable clinical impact, adding to the life expectancy or the quality of life of the patients involved. There is no doubt that part of the health advocates' greater persuasiveness is associated with their greater ability to assess Moroccan patients' nonverbal clues. They, as do health professionals, point out that advocates have less trouble assessing the atmosphere during an intervention and are more easily aware of the fact that patients do not understand what is being explained to them, or that they are unwilling to accept a piece of advice. This makes it possible to take patients' reactions into account. In addition, as members of the target group, health advocates are often aware of misconceptions that may affect the health behavior of their clients, such as the idea of some patients that the meningitis vaccination is injected directly into the brain (through the skull). Unlike the Belgian health professionals, health advocates are able to make sense of what they overhear in waiting rooms and can react to what is being said.

Providing Culturally Sensitive Care. All the improvements described so far ultimately have to do with the improved communication between health professionals and Moroccan patients. Apart from these, a number of other changes associated with the program were observed. In most cases, these changes are attempts to provide more culturally sensitive care and to better adapt health care institutions and procedures to the presence of ethnic minority patients. At one hospital a room was provided for Muslim patients to make it possible for them to pray without being disturbed. A health advocate working at one of the mother and baby health care centers pointed out that many pregnant women, for religious reasons, did not show up for their prenatal visits during Ramadan. They did not want to undergo a vaginal examination during this month. It was decided that in the future such examinations would no longer be carried out during Ramadan. Patients were informed of this fact and motivated to attend the prenatal clinic during the fast. In some hospitals, diets for diabetics were adapted to Moroccan eating habits. Health advocates were also able to resolve a number of conflicts between health staff and Moroccan patients and sometimes successfully defended their clients against insensitive and racist practices.

EFFECTS ON PATIENT SATISFACTION

Health care practitioners and health advocates alike point out that the program generally contributes to patient satisfaction. In very rare cases, patients do not want to have anything to do with the health advocate and are explicit about this during their intervention. In some cases, reference is made to their opinion that women should not work or that the way the health advocate is dressed is unacceptable to them. Many health advocates believe that some Moroccan men are afraid of the influence the advocates might have on their wives' ideas. We find support for this hypothesis in the fact that it is generally men who refuse health advocates admittance to their homes, even when their wives seem to be willing to let them in.

Most first-generation clients of the mother and baby health care centers tell us that the program contributes to their satisfaction with care. This also holds true for second-generation clients who master neither Dutch nor French. Surprisingly, most of these clients point out that their husbands are also very acceptable to them as interpreters, although we have evidence that their husbands' skills in Dutch and/or French are not very high. A factor that might be at play here is the fact that they are accustomed to health care delivered with minimal or very poor-quality communication.

Most second-generation clients tell us that they do not find the intervention of the health advocates useful to them. Two of them even state that they prefer not to have the health advocate around because they consider them to be an intrusion upon their privacy.

None of the hospital patients object to the presence of the health advocate. Eight of the eleven hospital patients we interviewed described the presence and interventions of the health advocate as very valuable. Remarkably, health advocates had only interpreted for two of these patients. Patients say they feel more at ease at the hospital thanks to the health advocate, whom they describe as the only person taking time to talk to them. In some cases, health advocates went to Belgian health professionals to collect information about messages their clients had not understood. For some patients, the health advocate was the only person in the hospital with whom they could communicate. Such patients value talking with the health advocate very highly.

Problems Associated with the Introduction of the Program

THRESHOLDS TO COMMUNICATION

Health advocates point out that health professionals are insufficiently aware of the complexities of translating messages from and to their Moroccan clients. They note the difficulty of translating biomedical terms into a language in which, in many cases, no equivalent terms exist. If such terms do exist, their clients often do not know them or are not familiar with the phenomena to which they refer (e.g., organs and technical equipment). In order to clarify patients' descriptions of symptoms, health advocates must probe their responses until they have sufficient information to answer the health professionals' questions. In many cases, concepts have to be explained to the client. In addition, some questions should not be asked in the presence of members of the opposite sex, for example, or should not be asked in a direct way (without some kind of an introduction or the use of euphemistic vocabulary). All of these factors may considerably slow down the consultation process, which frequently leads to irritation on the part of the health professionals. They claim that the amount of information they get with the assistance of the health advocate is not commensurate with the time needed to collect it.

We observe, as have other authors before us (Putsch 1985), that health advocates do not often translate literally, and they only recount to the health professional what they consider to be the gist (or what is medically relevant) of the exchange with the client. It is, however, unlikely that they possess the necessary skills to distinguish between medically relevant and irrelevant material. As Faust and Drickey (1986) have noted, it is hard for health advocates to determine the extent to which contextual information is relevant to clinical diagnosis. Short translations of patient statements may also be part of a strategy of implicit advocacy in the interest of the health professional—in other words, to make the consultation proceed smoothly and quickly (O'Neil 1989). Unfortunately, this strategy may lead to misinterpretation, ambiguity, and confusion.

Clients sometimes explicitly ask the health advocate not to translate certain statements to the health professional. This further adds to the fragmented and incomplete view the health professional may get of the patient's situation. When health advocates judge a statement to be highly relevant to the medical encounter, they sometimes successfully motivate their clients to give them the permission to recount their story to the health professional.

A central problem associated with the program is the lack of training of the health professionals in how to cooperate with the health advocates. Only one group of health professionals (the social nurses working for the mother and baby health care centers) have received extensive training in this respect. In many cases, health advocates and health professionals have never discussed how they view their cooperation: how literally the health advocates should translate, what the advocates will do when they consider certain questions to be inappropriate, and so forth. Because of the ever-present time pressures, health advocates and health professionals hardly ever get a chance to discuss problems experienced during their work. This situation frequently leads to irritation on both sides and stress on the part of the health advocate.

These problems are reinforced by health professionals' lack of insight into the complexities of cross-cultural communication and into the importance of cultural meanings associated with illnesses and the care delivery process.

In the hospitals we find consistent evidence that many health professionals do not rely on health advocates when they encounter a language or cultural barrier. They sometimes prefer to work with informal interpreters (family members, friends of the patient) or with the Moroccan cleaning person. In the literature, consensus exists that such strategies should be avoided, because the informal interpreters lack the necessary skills and because it is unlikely that sensitive themes will be discussed in their presence (Saldov and Chow 1994, Haffner 1992). Health profession-als find it easier to work with informal interpreters because they are immediately available. In some of the larger hospitals, some health pro-fessionals are not even aware of the existence of the health advocacy pro-gram. Another problem is that health advocates are often not present at the hospital when they are needed because, for example, the health advo-cate only works half a day a week at the hospital. All these factors lead to a situation in which meetings between patient, health advocate, and health professional are relatively rare. We find that health advocates are rarely present at times when their interventions could probably affect the quality of care most, such as when an anamnesis is taken or when pa-tients are undergoing examinations.

THE IMPACT OF BIOGRAPHICAL AND PSYCHOLOGICAL FACTORS

We observe that health advocates sometimes refuse to translate certain questions for their clients because they consider them inappropriate. This is particularly the case with questions about the personal lives of their clients (e.g., those relating to marital relationships). Questions about their clients' marital relationships and family life were in a number of cases not translated because the health advocates considered them un-acceptable intrusions on their clients' privacy (or felt that they would be perceived as such) and because they were opposed to "emancipationist"/assimilationist tendencies implicit in the questions.[2] Some health advo-cates argue that health professionals "want to change their culture." Some are also afraid of the possible reactions of the husbands of their clients when such questions are asked and fear that, as a result of these, they will be unable to continue their work in the future.

Evidence from our material suggests that the (un)willingness of some health advocates to translate questions of the type described above is strongly related to their attitudes toward their own cultural heritage (es-pecially to aspects related to their gender roles) and to their attitudes toward the Flemish community. Health advocates holding traditional Moroccan views on gender roles and having positive attitudes toward their own ethnic group tend to have more problems asking questions about their clients' private lives and to be less eager to promote contra-ception, for example. On the other hand, they are often very willing to discuss traditional therapies with their clients and health professionals and may go to great lengths to make arrangements, for example, for a traditional healing session to take place at the hospital. Health advocates holding views closer to these of most Flemish health professionals are sometimes even more eager than the health professionals to "emancipate" their women clients and to improve their situations through the promotion of contraception, for example. On the other hand, some authors have pointed out that such health advocates may be unwilling to discuss matters with heavy cultural overtones (e.g., folk remedies), because they do not wish to be associated with them (Putsch 1985).

A number of authors argue that health advocates, or "culture brokers," like many other second-generation immigrants, may wish to "pass" to the majority group, to escape what is perceived to be a negative self-identity (De Vos 1975, Lutz 1991). The working situation of health advocates (working together with Flemish health professionals who have more power, higher status, and more knowledge than they have) is in many ways a small-scale replica of ethnic relations in Flemish society at large. As such, it may reinforce the wish to pass. Lutz argues that the training to become an advocate has a similar effect (Lutz 1991). These processes affect health advocates' willingness to represent the viewpoints of their clients and make some of them less sensitive to the values and belief systems of their group. This may be why explanatory models, patients' conceptions of their health problems, and folk remedies are rarely discussed between health advocates and health professionals. The fact that some health professionals—and this is especially true for the medical doctors— do not often have the time to discuss cultural factors that may be relevant to the delivery of health care (or have repeatedly shown a lack of interest in such matters) contributes to this situation. Other authors have observed that the presence and interventions of health advocates do not necessarily lead to more attention for patients' conceptions of illness and treatment or for other cultural aspects of the provision of care (O'Neil 1989).

Finally, it should be noted that not fewer than five out of twenty-one Moroccan health advocates have sought professional help for psychological problems they believe to be associated with their work during the last year. As we have already pointed out, the situation of many of these advocates already makes them psychologically vulnerable. However, there is no doubt that the stress associated with the dual loyalty of the health advocate (to their clients and to the health professionals) may add to their psychological vulnerability, as may be the case with the confrontation of the negative views held by some Flemish health professionals and the aggressive reactions of some traditional clients. Health advocates are generally believed to be at a high risk for the development of burnout syndrome as a result of the stress associated with their work (Lutz 1991, Downing 1992).

CULTURE BROKERAGE

In general, health advocates are not often asked to provide information on cultural matters by most groups of health professionals with whom they are working. The social nurses working in mother and baby health care centers are an exception to this rule, probably because they spend more time with the health advocates (walking or driving together to pay home visits to their clients). A striking discrepancy exists between the interest of many health professionals in general cultural information and the nearly complete absence of attention to cultural factors during concrete interventions with individual patients. As a response to health professionals' need for general information on Moroccan patients' culture, special training sessions have been organized by some health advocates and the organizations for which they work. Such training sessions may be very useful, as most health professionals have received no formal training whatsoever on working with ethnic minority patients.[3] General information may, however, lead to the development or reinforcement of stereotypical views of ethnic minority patients. It may also reinforce health professionals' tendency to attribute problems experienced with such patients to their culture, which is often misleadingly viewed as monolithic and as a nearly exact replica of the culture of the country of origin (Van Dijk 1989).

Health advocates point out that it is not always easy for them to answer health professionals' questions about cultural matters. Their knowledge is generally limited to "how things are done and viewed in their own family." Whether they are familiar with certain types of folk remedies or forms of traditional Moroccan medicine, for example, is highly dependent upon accidental, biographical factors. Many of them are afraid to disseminate false information about Islam to health professionals. They try to study the Koran or scholarly works on Islam in order to be able to come up with the right answers. This strategy may be misleading, because Islam, as it is lived in the Moroccan community in Belgium, differs in many respects from official Islam. In addition, one may wonder whether Islam as strongly affects the delivery of health care as is suggested by the number of questions asked about it by health professionals.

ADVOCACY

Due to their own low status, explicit advocacy on behalf of their clients is very difficult for health advocates. Whether it is possible at all depends on, among other things, the attitudes of the health professionals with whom the health advocates are working and on their own assertiveness. O'Neil (1989) has argued that in order to be able to advocate for their clients, health advocates must occupy a position in the sociopolitical structure of the institution that enables them to challenge authority. This is not the case for the Flemish advocates. Unfortunately, many health advocates are also very unsure of themselves, especially when working at the hospitals. In addition, one may wonder whether health advocates always possess the necessary skills to judge what should be done for their clients.

Conclusions and Recommendations

This study indicates that the health advocacy program may result in an important improvement in the quality of care delivered to Moroccan patients, if adequate use is made of the health advocates' services. We find some evidence that the interventions of health advocates may also positively affect the health status of their clients.

Many factors, however, hamper the program's effectiveness. These problems are mainly associated with the complexity of cross-cultural communication and interpreting, psychological and biographical characteristics of the advocates, a lack of knowledge and skills in cooperating with health advocates on the part of health professionals, and the low status of the advocates.

To improve the effectiveness of this and similar programs, it is essential to increase health professionals' insight into the complexities of intercultural communication and interpreting and into the benefits of finding out patients' explanatory models of illness and treatment during patient encounters. As long as health professionals lack this insight, there is a real danger that health advocates will remain low-qualified health workers who filter information, as dictated by Western biomedicine, down to members of their community, as has been argued by Anderson (1986). It must be clear from our analysis that health advocates are in no position to challenge health professionals' agendas. In addition, it is crucial that health advocates and health professionals are jointly trained and learn how to work together.

To make it possible for health advocates to advocate in the interests of their clients, it is necessary that they occupy sociopolitical positions that enable them to challenge medical authority. Procedures ought to be developed that make it possible for the health advocates to assess what their clients' best interests are. These should certainly include conferring with independent health professionals, as health advocates lack the skills to judge what is medically necessary for their clients.

During the training of health advocates, sufficient attention should be paid to the influence of psychological and biographical processes on the way health advocates perform their tasks. Health advocates must receive adequate support to prevent them from developing burnout syndrome.

The efficiency and effectiveness of the program in hospitals would benefit enormously from a computerized patient check-in system that simultaneously alerts the advocacy service. Advocates should be on call to assist clients with a language need for these health care interventions. As long as health advocates are only relatively rarely present at the hospitals, and as long as health professionals do not systematically rely on their services, the effect on the quality of care will be very limited.

Finally, it should be noted that the introduction of health advocacy programs can only be a (small) part of a health policy aimed at the improvement of ethnic minorities' health status. Similar programs in England have been criticized by members of the ethnic communities for their deficit models of health inequalities, which implicitly blame their culture for the failure of the services to deliver suitable care. They claim that such programs are not free from a victim-blaming ideology and do not take into account the material implications for health status of racial and class disadvantages (e.g., the effects of poverty) (Rocheron 1988). Results of epidemiological research indicate that the health status of ethnic minorities will be only marginally improved as long as their unfavorable socioeconomic position is not improved (Ahmad 1989).

Acknowledgments

The authors would like to thank all the health advocates, health professionals, and patients who were interviewed for this study. We are grateful to Ms. Malika Abbad and Ms. Fatiha Hamidi (interpreters/interviewers), whose contributions to this study can hardly be overestimated. Finally, we would like to thank Dr. Ri De Ridder, chairman of the Health Advocacy Project, for his enthusiasm for our undertaking.

Notes

1. Because of financial and time constraints, we were only able to study the effects of the introduction of Moroccan (and not of Turkish) health advocates, and these only in two health care settings: mother and baby health care centers and hospitals.

2. Two examples of such questions are: Are you allowed to go out on your own? Does your husband help you with the education of the kids?

3. More than twenty years after the arrival of most Moroccan and Turkish immigrants, it still happens that health professionals working in hospitals serving large Moroccan and Turkish clienteles claim that Moroccans and Turks speak the same language and that the two countries are "virtually identical."

References

Ahmad, W. I. 1989. "Policies, Pills, and Political Will: A Critique of Policies to Improve the Health Status of Ethnic Minorities." *Lancet* 8630: 148–150.

———. 1992. "Race, Disadvantage, and Discourse: Contextualising Black People's Health." In W. I. Ahmad, ed., *The Politics of "Race" and Health.* Bradford: Race Relations Research Unit, University of Bradford and Bradford and Ilkley Community College, pp. 7–38.

Andersen, M. L. 1993. "Studying across Difference: Race, Class, and Gender in Qualitative Research." In J. H. Stanfield and R. M. Dennis, eds., *Race and Ethnicity in Research Methods.* Newbury Park, Calif.: Sage, pp. 39–52.

Anderson, J. M. 1986. "Ethnicity and Illness Experience: Ideological Structures and the Health Care Delivery System." *Social Science and Medicine* 22: 1277–1283.

De Muynck, A. 1990. "Waar wonen Ali en Fatima en welke problemen hebben ze met onze Belgische geneeskunde?" [Where do Ali and Fatima Live and Which Problems Do They Face in Belgian Health Care?]. *Acta Medica Catholica* 4: 29–40, 79–80.

De Vos, G. 1975. "Ethnic Pluralism: Conflict and Accommodation." In G. De Vos and L. Romanucci-Ross, eds., *Ethnic Identity: Cultural Continuities and Change.* Palo Alto, Calif.: Mayfield, pp. 5–41.

Downing, B. T. 1992. "The Use of Bilingual/Bicultural Workers as Providers and Interpreters." *International Migration* 30: 121–130.

Eppink, A. 1981. *Cultuurverschillen en communicatie: Problemen bij hulpverlening aan migranten in Nederland* [Cultural Differences and Communication: Problems with Care for Migrants in Holland]. Alphen aan den Rijn, Netherlands: Samson.

Faust, S., and R. Drickey. 1986. "Working with Interpreters." *Journal of Family Practice* 22: 131–138.

Haffner, L. 1992. "Translation Is Not Enough." *Western Journal of Medicine* 157: 255–259.

Hermans, P. 1991a. "Introduction: Quelques données de base concernant l'immigration marocaine en Belgique." In J. P. Gaudier and P. Hermans, eds., *Des belges marocains.* Brussels: De Boeck Université, pp. 1–12.

————. 1991b. "Aicha Qandicha à Bruxelles: Les troubles mentaux et leur traitement chez les immigrés marocains." In J. P. Gaudier and P. Hermans, eds., *Des belges marocains.* Brussels: De Boeck Université, pp. 200–265.

Kaufert, J. M., and W. W. Koolage. 1984. "Role Conflict among 'Culture Brokers': The Experience of Native Canadian Medical Interpreters." *Social Science and Medicine* 18: 283–286.

Lutz, H. 1991. *Welten verbinden: Türkische Sozialarbeiterinnen in den Niederlanden und der Bundesrepublik Deutschland.* Frankfurt am Main: Verlag für Interkulturelle Kommunikation.

O'Neil, J. D. 1989. "The Cultural and Political Context of Patient Dissatisfaction in Cross-Cultural Clinical Encounters: A Canadian Inuit Study." *Medical Anthropology Quarterly* 3: 325–344.

Peeters, R., and A. De Muynck. 1994. "De zorg voor allochtonen: De aandacht voor Marokkanen en Turken in de Vlaamse gezondheidszorg" [Health Care for Ethnic Minorities: The Attention for Turks and Moroccans in Flemish Health Care]. *Gezondheid: Theorie in Praktijk* 2: 84–100.

Putsch, R. W. 1985. "Cross-Cultural Communication: The Special Case of Interpreters in Health Care." *Journal of the American Medical Association* 254: 3344–3348.

Renaerts, M. 1991. "Rites de passage: L'exemple du marriage." In J. P. Gaudier and P. Hermans, eds., *Des belges marocains.* Brussels: De Boeck Université, pp. 57–93.

Rocheron, Y. 1988. "The Asian Mother and Baby Campaign: The Construction of Ethnic Minorities' Health Needs." *Critical Social Policy* 22: 4–23.

Rocheron, Y., R. Dickinson, and S. Khan. 1988. *Evaluation of the Asian Mother and Baby Campaign. I: Assessment of the Linkwork Program.* Leicester, England: Centre for Mass Communication Research, University of Leicester.

Saldov, M., and P. Chow. 1994. "The Ethnic Elderly in Metro Toronto Hospitals, Nursing Homes, and Homes for the Aged: Communication and Health Care." *International Journal of Aging and Human Development* 38: 117–135.

Van Dijk, R. 1989. "Cultuur als excuus voor een falende hulpverlening" [Culture as an Excuse for the Failure to Deliver Care]. *Medische Antropologie* 1: 131–143.

7

Health and Health Services Utilization in Spain among Labor Immigrants from Developing Countries

Antonio Ugalde

Spain historically has been a country of emigration. For centuries its surplus labor force moved to America, then during the early part of the twentieth century to North Africa, and more recently, from the 1950s to the mid-1970s, to member countries of the European Community.

The decade of the 1970s marked an important point in the history of contemporary migration in Spain: it was then that the number of Spaniards who emigrated to foreign countries decreased significantly while the number of foreigners who immigrated to Spain began to increase considerably. In 1975 there were 165,000 foreign residents in the country; by 1992 the number had grown to 415,000. To this number should be added foreigners with temporary work permits and an unknown number of illegal immigrants that varies widely from 70,000 to 294,000, according to different sources (Vidal Domínguez 1993, Aragón 1989, de Prada 1989). Because of its rapid growth in immigration, experts have classified Spain as a new center of immigration within the European Union, in spite of the fact that in 1990 Spain occupied the seventh place in number of foreign residents among the twelve member countries of the European Union at the time (Izquierdo Escribano 1990, Organization for Economic Cooperation and Development 1990).[1]

This paper is concerned exclusively with labor immigrants from developing countries and excludes political immigrants (exiles and refugees) and immigrants from industrial nations. It is worth noting that the largest number of foreign legal residents in Spain come from the European Union (almost 60 percent) (Blanco Fernández 1993). Of these, the largest percentage is from the United Kingdom. The migration process, health conditions and problems, accessibility to health services, and utilization issues are entirely different among the three types of migrants:

those from industrial nations, labor migrants from developing nations, and political immigrants (Bourdillon et al. 1991, Holtzman and Bornemann 1990).

In Spain labor immigration is likely to keep increasing as the economic gaps between nations continue to widen (Fielding 1993, López García 1993, Actis, de Prada, and Pereda 1993, Salt 1992, Callovi 1993). There is probably little that the immigration policies of the country and of the European Union could do to reverse this trend (Actis, de Prada, and Pereda 1993, Archdeacon 1992, Martin 1992). Spain is only a few miles away from Morocco, and hundreds of thousands of Moroccans cross the peninsula back and forth from Europe in the yearly visits to their homes. Spain also has close cultural and historical bonds with Latin America and maintains double nationality privileges with a number of Latin American countries.

The fastest-growing group of immigrants in Spain is from Morocco, but given the large number of immigrants without documents, it is difficult to estimate their numbers. Before the amnesty of 1991 it was estimated that there were 68,000 undocumented migrants from the Maghreb; in 1991 about 48,142 sought legal status through the amnesty program.[2] To give a sense of the growth of the group, we can use the official estimates of foreign residents (these exclude nationalized and undocumented immigrants). In 1966 there were only 836 foreign residents from the Maghreb, but by 1990 the number had grown to 17,670 (Blanco Fernández 1993, López García 1993).

Immigration, Acculturation, and Health

Before discussing the health conditions and the problems of accessibility to health services that labor immigrants encounter in Spain, it is useful to clarify that the term *immigrant* has multiple meanings. First, it can refer only to first-generation migrants, those who were born in a foreign country, regardless of their legal status today (nationalized, resident, temporary worker, illegal, refugee/exile). At times the term also includes second-generation migrants, the children of the first-generation migrants who were born in the country to which their parents immigrated. Frequently, these children are citizens of the country where they were born or could become so upon reaching adulthood. Strictly speaking, these persons are not immigrants and are not counted as such in the official statistics. Nevertheless, some migration studies include second-generation migrants because their acculturation process may be incomplete; second-generation migrants may have language difficulties, suffer discrimination, and experience cultural disintegration.

Health and illness behavior, utilization of health services, self-care attitudes, and health promotion and illness prevention behaviors of second-generation migrants are to some degree influenced by the parents' culture. In some cases—for example, in the case of children born to undocumented immigrants in Spain—their access to health services is limited. Furthermore, the literature suggests that second-generation migrants might have specific health problems caused by the very process of acculturation, particularly when acculturation takes place in the midst of social marginalization (Verdonk 1982).

Levels of acculturation of first-generation immigrants vary widely. Variables that affect acculturation include age at immigration, problems of language acquisition, and affinity between the culture of the country or region of origin and the receiving society. From an economic or demographic point of view, it may be important to quantify the number of first-generation immigrants in a country at a given time. From the point of view of health service delivery, it may be equally important to know the degree of acculturation of first- and second-generation immigrants. Unfortunately, in Spain there are very few significant studies of acculturation. The number of second-generation migrants is very small, but some hospitals (Hospital de Mataró 1991) have reported significant increases in pediatrics due to an increasing number of second-generation immigrants.

Health Conditions

The first exhaustive study of Maghrebians in Spain was carried out by López García and his collaborators (1993) and contains a large amount of information on place of origin and destination, occupational situation and labor conditions, and social and demographic characteristics. A second important study of Moroccans, although limited to the Catalonian Autonomy, is by Colectivo IOE (Actis, Pereda, and de Prada 1994). Other immigrants have been less studied, with the exception of a large comprehensive study of immigrants in Madrid (Giménez Romero 1993) and studies of immigrant women that include women from several countries (Solé 1994, Marrodán et al. 1991). Health conditions and problems related to access to health services are only treated in passing in immigration research, and there are very few health-specific studies (Jansà and Villalbí 1995).

Information on the health conditions of a population can be obtained from the national health insurance centers and hospitals (attended morbidity), participant observation (observed morbidity), the evaluation that each person makes of his or her health conditions (self-reported morbidity), and clinical surveys of the population (clinical morbidity).

ATTENDED AND OBSERVED MORBIDITY

In Spain attended morbidity is not a very reliable method to measure the health status of immigrant populations because many immigrants are not covered by the national health insurance (Social Security) and therefore do not utilize its services. For example, a small nonrandom survey of African immigrants in Granada found that 53 percent of the ninety-four respondents had felt sick during the previous twelve months but decided not to go to health centers (Gómez Rodríguez 1992). This study, one of the few that focuses on health conditions and utilization, does not present information on the severity of the illnesses; therefore, it is not possible to compare utilization behaviors of foreign immigrants and nationals. In 1994 we carried out a small survey of Moroccan (n = 100) and Spanish (n = 100) construction workers in Madrid. We asked them if they had felt the need to visit a health center but did not do so.[3] The responses provided a measurement of unattended morbidity. About 31 percent of Moroccans did not go to health providers when they felt they should have, versus 22 percent of Spaniards.

In Spain there are a few studies that have examined the attended morbidity at clinics used by immigrants. For example, a study of agricultural workers in the Poniente Almeriense documented the high incidence of illnesses such as headaches, depression, allergies, and paresthesia, as well as high rates of poisonings from exposure to pesticides (between 1980 and 1991 there were 85,302 cases in the local hospital). It also found that safety and protective regulations were ignored by agricultural firms that hired immigrant workers (Parrón, González, and Mascaro 1993). The study also suggested that there may have been a relation between exposure to pesticides and increases in suicide and abortion rates.

Immigrants who work in agriculture without protective gear often work in poorly ventilated areas—for example, in greenhouses under plastic covers—which leads to a relatively high rate of accidents and poisonings from contact with chemicals, as well as respiratory, skin, and eye diseases (Cruz Roja ca. 1992). Accidents also occur when workers cannot read the instructions for equipment because they have limited knowledge of Spanish or are illiterate (Pumares 1993).

High levels of sexually transmitted diseases have been reported among Sub-Saharan Africans. In a hospital in the metropolitan area of Barcelona, almost 47 percent of all consultations between 1983 and 1987 (n = 430) at the department of dermatology were for sexually transmitted diseases (Hospital de Mataró 1991). HIV-1 increased from one case (the first reported) in 1987 to eighteen cases in 1990 (Hospital de Mataró 1991).

Yearly reports of attended morbidity at Red Cross clinics used by immigrants also provide some information about their health conditions and problems. A 1992 report about clinics used mostly by Africans states the following (Cruz Roja ca. 1992):

> In very general terms and in different percentages, we found communicable diseases that were out of control, imported diseases of difficult treatment at the health centers; work accidents that had not been reported and had not been treated in order to hide irregular labor conditions; illnesses caused by poor or inadequate diets, by meals based on canned foods or foods that were not in good conditions because of a lack of refrigeration or the absence of the most elementary hygiene, use of non-potable water. . . . Another factor of various pathologies is the type of work that these persons carry out and the conditions under which they labor.[4]

Living conditions have an impact on health conditions, but it should be noted that they vary considerably among immigrants according to social class and occupation. In general, the worst conditions are found among agricultural workers, in some shanty towns on the periphery of Madrid, and among Sub-Saharan Africans (Pérez Losada 1993). According to Pumares (1993) a relatively large percentage of Moroccans in Madrid live in shanty towns without water and electricity. Restrooms and showers are also scarce, and under these conditions "even legal migrants had problems in keeping basic hygiene and sanitation. Weather conditions affect their health negatively because of the poor housing conditions" (Pumares 1993). In a town in the agricultural region of Segria, 9 percent of households did not have restrooms, and 9 percent did not have running water. Overcrowding is also common. Thus, in Granada, there were 6.1 Africans per household, with an average of 2.8 rooms per household, and 62 percent of households were considered overcrowded. Under these conditions, there is little privacy, and the possibilities of accidents and skin diseases increase. These problems do not exist for the thousands of immigrant women who are employed as live-in maids in middle- and upper-class families.

SELF-REPORTED AND CLINICAL MORBIDITY

The concepts of health and illness are culturally bounded (Susser, Watson, and Hopper 1985). Cultural differences between the native population and foreign immigrants regarding the meaning of health and illness make it challenging to compare health conditions through self-reported morbidity. For example, in the last national health survey of Hispanics in the United States, it was found that there were statistically significant differences between those who used English and those who preferred to use Spanish in answering a Likert-scale question about their own health status. It was not clear if the differences responded to variations produced by the way some terms had been translated from English into Spanish, by different levels of acculturation, or by different health conditions.

In Spain a few studies have asked respondents to assess their own health conditions. In Granada 43 percent of the African immigrants reported that their health was not very good (*regular*), and 3 percent that it was bad. If we keep in mind that respondents were young adults and that labor migration tends to be selective, the above percentages suggests precarious health conditions, and, probably, a deterioration of health conditions after arrival in Spain. This view is also supported by de Vicente Abad (1993), according to whom the health conditions of Sub-Saharan Africans are determined more by conditions in which they find themselves in Spain (labor precariousness, illegality, and poor housing) than by the conditions at home in Africa.

In our study of construction workers we asked respondents the nature of the health problem that prompted the last medical consultation. The responses are presented in table 7.1. The table shows that a relatively large percentage of responses indicate that immigrants suffer mental and psychosomatic disorders: general malaise (12 percent), depression/anxiety (3 percent), dizziness (12 percent), headaches (15 percent), chest pains (14 percent), stomach aches (10 percent), weakness (1 percent). The total percentage of these conditions is 67, considerably higher than the 15 percent reported by the Spanish construction workers.

Our hypothesis is that immigration in Spain causes mental health problems and psychosomatic conditions. This view is supported by the study of African immigrants in Granada, where diagnosis during first

Table 7.1. Self-Identified Principal Symptoms (Last Medical Consultation), Moroccan and Spanish Construction Workers, Madrid, 1994 (percentages)

Symptoms	Moroccan Workers	Spanish Workers
Headaches	15	7
Chest pains	14	1
Dizziness	12	14
General malaise	12	2
Stomachaches	10	4
Wounds or injuries	10	13
Influenza	8	15
Aches of the joints	6	8
Backaches	3	4
Depression or anxiety	3	—
Weakness	1	—
Other	6	34
Total	100	99
n	(73)	(95)

consultations identified disorders such as gastric ulcers and other diseases of the digestive system, depressive disorders, insomnia, and headaches, all of which could be related to the stresses of immigration.

There is additional support for our hypothesis from a clinical survey of Latin American residents in Madrid. Marrodán, Herranz Gómez, and García Ruiz (1989: 38) found "prevalence of genitourinary, osteomuscular, endocrine, metabolic and nutritional problems, amenorrhea, hypertension and obesity increase after arrival. Some of these problems may be related to anxiety and stress, and be a response to activity and nutritional changes. We also observed a light increase of nervous system problems and accidents (falls, injuries, and fractures)."

The instability of employment and income (Pumares 1993), social and cultural marginalization (Páez 1993), family separation (Zapata de la Vega 1993), pressures to send money home (Gómez Rodríguez 1992, Jabardo Velasco 1993), racial discrimination (Celaya 1993, Solé 1992, Alvite 1995), and lack of documents are some conditions that could explain the mental and psychosomatic problems of immigrants in Spain.

Immigrants themselves link their social problems with worrying, as these quotes from immigrants attest (Gómez Rodríguez 1992):

- "If you have papers you are fine, otherwise you are worried . . . nervous."
- "I feel like in a jail, without a residence or a working permit."
- "There are many who cannot sleep, they think that they are not going to be given the papers, and if the police stop you . . . too many problems and you cannot sleep."
- "The only money left is to be sent to Africa, and this is the most important thing . . . the food for my children, my wife, my mother, my family."

The 1991 amnesty did not resolve the illegal condition of many immigrants, including those who could not apply because they did not have an employer (a condition to apply) or those whose request was denied (Jansà and Villalbí 1995, Ramírez 1993), or, of course, those who arrived illegally after 1991. In other words, five years after the amnesty, there continues to be a large number of illegal immigrants in Spain.

In sum, based on the literature in other countries (Bourdillon et al. 1991) and the sparse information available in Spain (Jansà and Villalbí 1995), it can be suggested that the health conditions of immigrants in this country are influenced by:

1. The high-risk conditions under which they work, their long hours of work, and in general the exploitation they are exposed to (Actis, Pereda, and de Prada 1994). Risks at work increase with the deterioration of the mental health of the workers (Almeida 1985).
2. Labor and legal instability/illegality, which produce anxiety and other mental health and psychosomatic problems (de Vicente Abad 1993).
3. Family separation and the absence of psychosocial support precisely when immigrants are exposed to anxiety and racism and feel pressures to send money to their families at home (Torres 1995). Family separation also has a negative impact on nutrition. Meals are poorly prepared and are frequently based on canned foods, which, together with substandard housing (lack of hygiene and refrigeration) and poverty, lead to nutritional and gastric disorders.
4. The use of controlled drugs. According to a report of the Red Cross (Cruz Roja ca. 1992), there have been cases of immigrants who took anabolic drugs and male hormones as energy boosters to be able to work harder and obtain additional income.

5. Overcrowding and poor living conditions (Comisión de las Asociaciones y ONGs 1992).
6. Cultural values that at times are incompatible with norms of hygiene and nutrition.

Accessibility and Utilization of Health Services

Studies in several countries indicate that immigrants utilize health services less than native populations (Chávez, Cornelius, and Jones 1985, Montiero 1977, Nagi and Haavio-Manilla 1980). In Spain we do not know if this is also the case, nor have we fully studied the types of services used by immigrants.

Several immigration studies in Spain give a simplistic two-category classification of immigrants and their access to health services (Pumares 1993, Páez 1993). According to them, all immigrants with work permits and their dependents have, like other Spaniards, access to free health services offered by the national health insurance (Seguridad Social), and undocumented labor immigrants do not. Unfortunately, this is not the case (Comisión de las Asociaciones y ONGs 1992, Asociación de Mujeres Dominicanas en España 1992). For example, many self-employed immigrants who have immigration papers, and therefore work permits, cannot afford to pay the premiums required by Social Security. Legal discrimination also plays a part. Spaniards who earn less than the minimum salary (whose annual income is lower than the interprofessional salary) and Spanish indigents have the right to utilize Social Security health services without paying the health insurance premiums, but legal immigrants who are indigent or earned less than the minimum salary do not (Real Decreto 1088 of 1989). Finally, there is an unknown number of immigrants who are not covered by Social Security insurance because their employers fail to pay their contribution to Social Security as required by law. Immigrants are afraid of demanding that their employers make the contribution for fear of being fired and as a result losing not only their income but also their permit to stay in Spain. These realities translate into limited access and coverage, which have been documented in a few studies, but there are no large-sample studies that quantify the number of immigrants who are not able to use health services when in need.

In the Madrid study of construction workers, we asked those who had felt the need to go to a health center and did not do so the reasons why they did not use health services. As shown in table 7.2, 33 percent of the

Moroccan sample responded that they were afraid because of their illegal status or because they did not have Social Security coverage, whereas only 6 percent of Spanish workers did not have Social Security coverage. Fear of missing work was the second reason (27 percent), and there were no Spaniards in this category. Illegal immigrants were probably afraid of missing work and being fired for it. Legal residents might also fear the possibility of losing their jobs, because in Spain unemployed immigrants lose their legal residency status. Spaniards do not express this fear because, according to labor laws, workers can take a paid leave for health reasons. Theoretically, legal Moroccan immigrants could invoke this law, but in practice they know that they could be fired almost at will; discrimination is a reality. Among Moroccan workers 23 percent felt that they did not have the time to go to a health center; among the Spaniards this is the largest category (89 percent), and it probably indicates that the health problems were not very severe. Lack of money was a barrier to access for 7 percent of Moroccans, and 10 percent had a negative experience during previous visits to health centers.

Immigrants not covered by Social Security receive primary health care from the Red Cross and other NGOs, from the emergency services of Social Security and other public institutions in emergencies, from municipal health clinics, and from private health providers. The Red Cross, under contract with the government, had provided health care to refugees and exiles for many years and in 1990 signed a contract with the Ministry of Social Welfare and began to offer primary health care to labor immigrants. It provides the services in a handful of health centers in seven provinces in areas where the immigrants concentrate. The Red Cross has found many difficulties in the provision of services: "it is hard to follow up patients and treat adequately those who require several consultations, access to specialized medicine is very limited, and there are severe laboratory and x-ray limitations" (Cruz Roja ca. 1992). This view is shared, as we will see, by users. Other institutions have also found difficulties in follow-up and have noted that many patients do not come for scheduled consultations. Thus, in Mataró (Hospital de Mataró 1991) in 1990, of 165 patients who had been scheduled for a first consultation, only 99 (60 percent) showed up and only 71 percent went to the hospital for the scheduled second consultation.

According to one study in Madrid, 24 percent of Latin Americans from the Southern Cone (Argentina, Uruguay, and Chile)—who generally enjoy higher socioeconomic status than most migrants from developing countries—did not have any type of health insurance; this per-

Table 7.2. Reasons for Not Using Health Services When in
Need of Care, Moroccan and Spanish Construction Workers,
Madrid, 1994 (percentages)

Reasons	Moroccan Workers	Spanish Workers
Fear because of lack of papers/ lack of Social Security papers	33	6
Fear of losing employment	27	—
Lack of time	23	89
Previous negative experiences	10	—
Lack of money	7	—
Did not want to spend money	—	6
Total	100	101
n	(30)	(18)

centage increased to 42 for the rest of Latin Americans (Marrodán, Herranz Gómez, and García Ruiz 1989). The latter percentage is similar to the one reported in Barcelona among Latin American users of social services of the Immigrant Diocesan Commission (CDM) (Actis, de Prada, and Pereda 1993). Among those who were not using the CDM, 25 percent received care at the indigent municipal services (Actis, de Prada, and Pereda 1993).

The amnesty has not ensured legalized immigrants access to health services. Jabardo Velasco (1993), in his study of Maghrebian immigrants in Orihuela, noted: "According to the data provided by the local unemployment office, about 50 percent of immigrants who had initiated the process to petition Amnesty had received between May and October of 1991 a work pre-contract in the agricultural sector. But we were informed by the labor union that these contracts—given by agricultural firms who employ immigrants regularly—were accepted by immigration officers but were not binding as a labor contract, and consequently did not provide social assistance or health coverage" (p. 280).

Besides the Red Cross, other NGOs—some of which are exclusively organized to assist immigrants—provide primary health services to immigrants not covered by Social Security. Because most NGOs' services are based on volunteer personnel and have very few resources (Cifuentes Mimosos 1993), some of them decided that they could better serve the needs of the immigrants if their efforts were directed at pressuring the public sector to offer these services. In some places their advocacy was successful (Páez 1993). For example, in Barcelona, the municipality reached an agreement with NGOs to provide medical assistance to immigrants regardless of their legal status. Similarly, in 1991, the Diocesan Delegation for Immigration and the health centers of the municipality of Madrid reached an agreement by which the health centers would provide health care to those immigrants who were registered in the municipality (this is a simple bureaucratic procedure). The agreement was well received by immigrants, who have used the services since then with the limitations that will be discussed later. But a similar agreement could not be obtained from the municipalities in the metropolitan area of Madrid (Pumares 1993).

A very small number of immigrants have private health insurance or go to private practitioners. This is the case of workers in some occupations, such as live-in maids, whose employers prefer to pay private health services because they are less expensive than the entire Social Security package, which includes health and retirement payments.

In sum, the primary health services offered by the Red Cross and other NGOs are limited, and only a small number of municipal health services provide health care on a regular basis to immigrants not covered by Social Security. There are no studies of the quality of care provided to immigrants, but some studies have noted the complaints voiced by immigrants about the precariousness and insufficiency of the services provided by the Red Cross (Páez 1993).

Access to specialized and hospital care is extremely limited for immigrants who are not covered by Social Security health insurance. In Madrid one hospital (Ramón y Cajal) has a department of tropical medicine and attends illegal immigrants who suffer from these diseases. A Red Cross hospital (King's Hospital) cares for refugees and immigrants with uncommon communicable diseases (Páez 1993). Only in emergencies are immigrants not covered by Social Security seen by specialists or interned in hospitals; all other cases remained untreated.

Payments for emergencies vary by autonomic government.[5] In Mataró in the first quarter of 1991 about 66 percent of consultations in the emergency department were classified as charity, 24 percent were covered by Social Security, 3 percent were paid by the patients themselves, and the rest (17 percent) by other sources such as NGOs (see table 7.3). The table also shows that Social Security coverage is much higher among Maghrebian immigrants than among Sub-Saharan Africans, a situation that is probably the case in other parts of Spain.

Table 7.3. Sources of Payment for Emergency Consultations,
January–April 1990 and 1991, Mataró, Barcelona (percentages)

Sources	Sub-Saharan Africans		Maghrebians		Total	
	1990	1991	1990	1991	1990	1991
Charitable	63	72	43	60	56	66
Social Security	19	19	36	30	26	24
Private	9	3	12	4	10	3
Other	8	6	8	7	8	6
Total	99	100	99	101	100	99

Source: Hospital de Mataró 1991.

But in Madrid when immigrants are hospitalized during emergencies they are requested after leaving the hospital to pay the costs, and social workers are asked by bewildered patients how they are supposed to be able to pay the bill (Pumares 1993). In Spain political leaders have not been as outspoken and cynical as their French counterparts, who claimed that in France health care could not be provided to immigrants because the country did not have enough resources to assist all the "disinherited" of the third world (Bourdillon et al. 1991), but the final consequences are the same.

Social Security physicians and nurses face a difficult ethical dilemma. On the one hand, their profession requires them to assist all persons in need regardless of their ability to pay, but on the other hand, there are institutional rules that restrict coverage to beneficiaries. At the primary care level, rules and regulations tend to be easily circumvented, but bureaucratic controls are rigorous at the hospital level and much more difficult to bend.

BARRIERS TO UTILIZATION OF SERVICES

One barrier to utilization is the perception that users have of the services. If patients feel that providers do not treat them properly, they will stop going to the services. It has been indicated that 10 percent of Moroccan construction workers had negative experiences, and other studies have mentioned complaints by immigrants about the way they were treated. De Vicente Abad (1993) reports the experience of a Senegalese patient who was very upset by the way he was treated at a Red Cross center: "When I went to the Red Cross they did not bother to listen to me, they do not care for you . . . here (at a private clinic) they do take care of me very well" (p. 303). A visit to a health center can also be a humiliating experience. For example, when immigrants go to the emergency room of Social Security clinics or hospitals, they may see themselves as asking for a favor or an alm.

Some authors have noted that immigrants from developing nations tend to delay going to health centers when they are sick, that they are not interested in learning about modern health and preventive practices, and that they are not willing to pay for medicines. These authors have suggested that "a modern health culture is entirely absent among [Moroccan] immigrants" (Pumares 1993, p. 184). Without denying that cultures (including those of economically advanced nations) have values that may not be entirely compatible with modern health principles, it is possible to explain the above health behaviors of immigrants. We have already noted that immigrants are fearful of visiting health centers because contacts with public institutions are perceived as risks for being detained (Cifuentes Mimosos 1993). It should be remembered that the yearly number of detentions and expulsions are high in Spain (37,700 and 5,700, respectively, in 1990); it is therefore understandable that immigrants would delay as much as possible any visits to public health centers.

Delays and lack of participation in educational programs may have been caused by the immigrants' lack of information, but health institutions and personnel are also poorly informed. According to the Red Cross,

> Immigrants are not the only ones who lack information; it may sound paradoxical but personnel who work in different offices of the public health administration also lack information. In this respect it should be mentioned that a provincial office of the Red Cross recently received a communication from the General Secretariat of the Social Security Health Services (INSALUD) in which it is affirmed that the Red Cross is responsible for the health care of foreign immigrants who have a temporary work permit because of a contract signed with the Ministry of Social Services (INSERSO), and this is not the case. (Cruz Roja ca. 1992)

As in other countries (see de Muynck, and Verrept and Louckx in this volume), in Spain language and cultural barriers are impediments to utilization. In Spain immigrants have complained that the patient-physician relationship is negatively influenced by communication problems that go beyond language. At times patients and physicians speak the same language but fail to communicate because they do not understand each other's culture (Putsch 1987). Pumares (1993) explains that a Red Cross clinic near Madrid (Boadilla) that was attended exclusively by Moroccan immigrants hired a Moroccan physician, but he could not communicate with his compatriots from the region of Rif, who speak a different language (Berber) and have a different culture. Communication problems have been detected in most studies (Hospital de Mataró 1991, Gómez Rodríguez 1992). In Granada, health administrators and providers, as well as clinical histories of African patients, revealed communication problems. According to the author of the study (Gómez Rodríguez 1992), "Cultural-linguistic barriers as well as legal-bureaucratic barriers result in lower efficiency and make more difficult diagnosis, follow up care, and treatment of health problems" (p. 75).

In Spain the need for special provisions to facilitate access and to improve the quality of care has yet to be considered. In the few cases where a health center has organized special health activities for immigrants, such as health education and preventive programs, the instructors were totally unaware of the needs and cultural differences of the audience. As a result, immigrants stopped attending the classes because the content was unrelated to their health problems (Pumares 1993), but instructors blame the "traditional" culture of Moroccans for the loss of interest.

For immigrants with few resources who are not covered by Social Security, the purchase of medicines becomes a barrier to following physicians' prescribed regimens. Sources of medicines vary: some are given free by NGOs and municipal clinics, and others are purchased. In Granada only 39 percent of respondents could purchase medicines; the rest had to depend on donations from NGOs, physicians, and friends. According to a Caritas officer, it is not uncommon that immigrants give up buying medicines because they need to send the money home (personal communication). Compliance with medical regimens is more problematic when patients are illiterate and provider and user do not speak the same language (Pumares 1993). Immigrants do not have easy access in Spain to the traditional therapeutic products that they used at home, which are sometimes very efficient in the treatment of some diseases.

Mobility also constitutes a barrier to adequate health care. Primary health care principles recommend continuity in the physician-family interaction, but it is difficult for immigrants who work in agriculture to maintain a steady relationship because they are constantly on the move. Moreno Torregrosa (1993), who studied Moroccan and Algerian immigrants in Valencia, remarked that "the main problem [in estimating the number of immigrants] is their great mobility. They go from one region to another according to work opportunities. Another problem is the fact that all of them are illegal, without a work and residence permit. They show up during working hours and disappear at night and weekends" (p. 242).

Conclusions

Labor immigration from developing countries is increasing in Spain at a fast pace, and all signs are that it will continue to do so in the next few years. The number of social, economic, and demographic studies on immigration is significant, but in the health area we have only a very partial understanding of immigrants' health conditions, barriers to and utilization of health services, and health and illness behaviors. The information that is scattered in passing in a number of migration studies and a few health studies uncovers a precarious health status and limited access to services, particularly to specialized and hospital care.

In addition to carrying out a national health survey of first- and second-generation immigrants that would provide an epidemiological profile, it is necessary to research specific health topics such as the health cost of immigration for Spain and for the immigrants themselves. The literature reviewed and our own work confirm that immigrants' labor conditions, family situations, discrimination and marginalization, and poor housing have serious negative effects on their health. Nutritional and digestive disorders, high levels of anxiety and depression, psychosomatic disorders, skin diseases, and accidents by poisoning are among the conditions mentioned by the studies. But there is a need for more detailed studies of morbidity by cause, which would allow, when required, legislative changes or stricter enforcement of existing laws. The morbidity patterns of the majority of immigrants in Spain reflect the social problems they encounter while trying to survive in the new home country rather than their health conditions before migration. In conclusion, we can tentatively say that labor immigrants in Spain provide cheap labor at the expense of their own health.

At the health delivery level, it would be useful to detail barriers to access, in particular to secondary and tertiary services, and find solutions that would require a more humanitarian approach and legislative changes. The physician-patient relationship merits special attention in determining the understanding that the providers have of the sociocultural context of their immigrant patients, the problems patients encounter in expressing themselves, and their degree of understanding of physicians' advice. These findings should translate into training programs for personnel attending immigrants and for identifying special provisions.

To better serve Moroccan immigrants, who constitute the largest national immigrant group in Spain, Spanish scholars should invite their Moroccan counterparts to form research teams with them to facilitate a better understanding of the cultural contexts. Together they could prepare preventive and promotional programs that would be culturally more attractive to this immigrant group.

Acknowledgments

I would like to express my appreciation to the Inter-University Program for Latino Research for a small grant to organize the International Migration and Human Rights Project at the University of Texas at Austin. As part of the project, I commissioned the health questionnaires given to Moroccan construction workers in Madrid. The Institute of Latin American Studies of the University of Texas at Austin assisted me with a 1993 Summer Research Grant to conduct health research among Latin American immigrants in Spain, and in 1996 the College of Liberal Arts and the Center for Middle Eastern Studies of the same university provided support for the preparation of this paper.

Notes

1. Italy also has been considered a new immigration country for the same reasons. Some authors have noted that Spain and Italy have the lowest fertility rates in the world at a time when there is a population explosion in northern Africa. The rapidly increasing flow of immigrants from North Africa to Spain and Italy has been attributed in part to the opposite population dynamics of the two regions.

2. A detailed account of the 1991 amnesty, or *regularización* (as it is known in Spain), can be found in Aragón Bombín and Chozas Pedrero 1993.

3. All direct quotations have been translated by the author.

4. The survey of construction workers was carried out by the Colectivo IOE (Madrid). I was allowed to add to their questionnaire a dozen questions about health. The survey was administered during November and early December of 1994. Moroccan field-workers interviewed Moroccan workers; the questionnaire was translated into Arabic, but some field-workers were native Berber speakers and used Berber with some respondents. The questionnaire was pretested, and changes were introduced as required. The metropolitan area of Madrid was divided into four geographical sections (north, south, east, and

west), and construction sites were identified in each section. Fifty respondents (25 Spaniards and 25 Moroccans) were selected in the sites in each section. Interviews were conducted at the sites during or after working hours. A description of the methodology and research findings can be found in Actis, Pereda, and de Prada 1995.

5. Spain is divided into seventeen autonomic or regional governments that correspond to linguistic and historical regions. Each government enjoys different degrees of fiscal and politico-administrative autonomy (known as *competencia*) from the central government.

References

Actis, W., M. A. de Prada, and C. Pereda. 1993. *La inmigración extranjera en Catalunya.* Barcelona: Institut Català d'Estudis Mediterranis.

Actis, W., C. Pereda, and M. A. de Prada. 1994. *Marroquíes en Catalunya: ¿Nuevos catalanes?* Barcelona: Institut Català d'Estudis Mediterranis.

————. 1995. "Inmigrantes y mercados de trabajo en España." 2 vols. Madrid: Report prepared for the Dirección General de Migraciones, Ministerio de Asuntos Sociales.

Almeida, D. 1985. "Les sinostroses chez les immigrés." *Revue de Medicine du Travail* 3: 37–41.

Alvite, J. P. 1995. "Racismo e inmigración." In J. P. Alvite, ed., *Racismo, antirracismo e inmigración.* Donostia, Spain: Tercera Prensa–Hirugarren Prentsa.

Aragón, R. 1989. "Hacia una política activa de inmigración." *Revista de Economía y Sociología del Trabajo* 11: 97–108.

Aragón Bombín, R., and J. Chozas Pedrero. 1993. *La regularización de inmigrantes durante 1991–1992.* Madrid: Ministerio de Trabajo y Seguridad Social.

Archdeacon, T. J. 1992. "Reflections on Immigration to Europe in Light of U.S. Immigration History." *International Migration Review* 26: 525–548.

Asociación de Mujeres Dominicanas en España. 1992. "Dominicanas en España (realidad y testimonio)." Unpublished report. Madrid.

Blanco Fernández de Valderrama, C. 1993. "The New Host: The Case of Spain." *International Migration Review* 26: 169–181.

Bourdillon, F., P. Lombrail, M. Antoni, J. Benrekassa, R. Bennegadi, M. Leloup, C. Huraux-Rendu, and J. C. Scotto.1991. "La santé des populations d'origine etrangere en France." *Social Science and Medicine* 32: 1219–1228.

Callovi, G. 1993. "Regulation of Immigration in 1993: Pieces of the European Community Jig-saw Puzzle." *International Migration Review* 26: 353–372.

Celaya, C. 1993. "La vuelta a los desprecios: Algunas consideraciones sobre la xenofobia en la España de los noventa." In B. López García, ed., *Inmigración magrebí en España: El retorno de los moriscos.* Madrid: Editorial Mapfre, pp. 305–328.

Chavez, J. R., W. Cornelius, and W. O. Jones. 1985. "Mexican Immigrants and the Utilization of U.S. Health Services." *Social Science and Medicine* 21: 93–102.

Cifuentes Mimosos, N. 1993. "Inmigración y salud: Relaciones de los inmigrantes con el sistema sanitario." Paper presented at the workshop "Salud e Inmigración," June 22–23, 1993, Nerja, Málaga.

Comisión de las Asociaciones y ONGs de las Comarcas de Girona. 1992. "Girona: Cincuenta propuestas sobre inmigración." Unpublished report. Gerona, Spain.

Cruz Roja. Circa 1992. *Ponencia sobre la situación sanitaria de la población inmigrante.* Madrid: Departamento de Actividades y Servicios. (Unpublished report).

de Prada, M. A. 1989. "España, país de emigración a país de inmigración." In M. A. Roque, ed., *Els moviments humans en el Mediterrani.* Barcelona: Institut Català d'Estudis Mediterranis.

de Vicente Abad, J. 1993. "Los inmigrantes negroafricanos en la Comunidad Autónoma de Madrid." In C. Giménez Romero, ed., *Inmigrantes extranjeros en Madrid. Vol. 2: Estudios monográficos de colectivos inmigrantes.* Madrid: Imprenta Comunidad de Madrid, pp. 251–336.

Fielding, A. 1993. "Migration, Institutions, and Politics: The Evolution of European Migration Policies." In R. King, ed., *Mass Migration in Europe: The Legacy and the Future.* London: Belhaven Press, pp. 40–61.

Giménez Romero, C., ed. 1993. *Inmigrantes extranjeros en Madrid.* 2 vols. Madrid: Imprenta Comunidad de Madrid.

Gómez Rodríguez, A. J. 1992. "Necesidades de salud y utilización de servicios sanitarios por los inmigrantes africanos en Granada." Master's thesis, Escuela Andaluza de Salud Pública (Granada).

Holtzman, W. H., and T. H. Bornemann, eds. 1990. *Mental Health of Immigrants and Refugees.* Austin: Hogg Foundation for Mental Health, University of Texas at Austin.

Hospital de Mataró. 1991. Untitled report. Mataró, Spain.

Izquierdo Escribano, A. 1992. *La inmigración en España, 1980–1990.* Madrid: Ministerio de Trabajo y Seguridad Social.

Jabardo Velasco, M. 1993. "Inmigrantes magrebíes en la agricultura: La Vega Baja del Segura (Orihuela)." In B. López García, ed., *Inmigración magrebí en España: El retorno de los moriscos.* Madrid: Editorial Mapfre, pp. 267–290.

Jansà, J. M., and J. R. Villalbí. 1995. "La salud de los inmigrantes y la atención primaria." *Atención Primaria* 15: 320–327.

López García, B., ed. 1993. *Inmigración magrebí en España: El retorno de los moriscos.* Madrid: Editorial Mapfre.

Marrodán, M. D., Y. Herranz Gómez, and C. M. García Ruiz. 1989. "La inmigración de iberoamericanos en Madrid: Consecuencias sociobiológicas." Unpublished report. Department of Animal Biology, Universidad Complutense, Madrid.

Marrodán, M. D., I. David, C. Sancho, M. C. Santamarta, and A. Relaño. 1991. *Mujeres del tercer mundo en España: Modelo migratorio y caracterización sociodemográfica*. Madrid: Ediciones Fundación CIPIE (Estudios sobre Mujer y Migración).

Martin, P. L. 1992. "Trade, Aid, and Migration." *International Migration Review* 26: 162–172.

Montiero, L. 1977. "Immigrants without Care." *Society* 14: 38–42.

Moreno Torregrosa, P. 1993. "Argelinos y marroquíes en Valencia: La aportación argelina a la inmigración en España." In B. López García, ed., *Inmigración magrebí en España: El retorno de los moriscos*. Madrid: Editorial Mapfre, pp. 241–252.

Nagi, S. Z., and E. Haavio-Manilla. 1980. "Migration, Health Status, and Utilization of Health Services." *Society, Health, and Illness* 2: 174–193.

Organization for Economic Cooperation and Development. 1990. "Situación actual en el campo de las migraciones." Unpublished report. Paris and Geneva.

Páez, M. T. 1993. "Cultura marroquí y migración." In C. Giménez Romero, ed., *Inmigrantes extranjeros en Madrid. Vol. 2: Estudios monográficos de colectivos inmigrantes*. Madrid: Imprenta Comunidad de Madrid, pp. 225–251.

Parrón, T., M. C. González, and M. L. Mascaro. 1993. "Estudio de los riesgos ocasionados por el uso de plaguicidas en la zona del Poniente Almeriense." Paper presented at the workshop "Salud e Inmigración," June 22–23, 1993, Nerja, Málaga.

Pérez Losada, D. 1993. "Análisis de los expedientes de extranjeros atendidos en la delegación diocesana de inmigrantes (años 1986–1991)." In C. Giménez Romero, ed., *Inmigrantes extranjeros en Madrid. Vol. 1: Panorama general y perfil sociodemográfico*. Madrid: Imprenta Comunidad de Madrid, pp. 461–497.

Pumares, P. 1993. "La inmigración marroquí." In C. Giménez Romero, ed., *Inmigrantes extranjeros en Madrid. Vol. 2: Estudios monográficos de colectivos inmigrantes*. Madrid: Imprenta Comunidad de Madrid, pp. 119–224.

Putsch, R. W. 1987. "La communication transculturelle." *Migration Santé* 52: 4–10.

Ramírez, A. 1993. "La inmigración magrebí en la Cataluña agrícola: Marroquíes en el litoral catalán." In B. López García, ed., *Inmigración magrebí en España: El retorno de los moriscos*. Madrid: Editorial Mapfre, pp. 225–240.

Salt, J. 1992. "The Future of International Migration." *International Migration Review* 26: 1977–1111.

Solé, C. 1992. "Trabajadores extranjeros en Cataluña: ¿Integración o racismo?" *Alfoz* 91–92: 162–170.

Solé, C. 1994. *La mujer inmigrante*. Madrid: Instituto de la Mujer, Ministerio de Asuntos Sociales.

Susser, M. W., W. Watson, and K. Hopper. 1985. *Sociology in Medicine*. Oxford: Oxford University Press.

Torres, R. 1995. *Yo, Mohamed. Historias de inmigrantes en un país de emigrantes.* Madrid: Ediciones Temas de Hoy.

Verdonk, A. L. 1982. "The Children of Immigrants in the Netherlands: Social Position and Implied Risks for Mental Health." In R. C. Nann, ed., *Uprooting and Surviving.* Boston: D. Reidel.

Vidal Domínguez, M. J. 1993. *Movilidad espacial del colectivo magrebí: Madrid, ¿ciudad de tránsito o de permanencia?* In B. López García, ed., *Inmigración magrebí en España: El retorno de los moriscos.* Madrid: Editorial Mapfre, pp. 331–354.

Zapata de la Vega, J. 1993. "Aspectos de la situación legal de los magrebíes en la comarca de L'Horta (Valencia)." In B. López García, ed., *Inmigración magrebí en España: El retorno de los moriscos.* Madrid: Editorial Mapfre, pp. 253–266.

8

Cycle and Reproductive Patterns among Immigrant Women in Spain

Consuelo Prado Martínez, María D. Marrodán Serrano,
Ángeles Sánchez-Andrés, Esperanza Gutiérrez Redomero,
Paula Acevedo Cantero, and Julia Sebastián Herranz

Traditionally, international migration has been characterized as a male phenomenon, but during the last decades female and male mobility have become very similar. Today female migration often is unrelated to family reunification, and with more frequency women migrate on their own and have established their own migration networks (Zeverín 1985, Marrodán et al. 1991a, David 1990). In recent times female migration has become more important, a fact that is reflected in the increasing number of studies of migrant women (Tapinos 1990, Chapman 1991, Bolzman 1993).

In Spain, immigrant women from developing countries tend to be young: about two thirds are under fifty years of age, and a little more than half of them are within reproductive age. Among this population, about 20 percent are under fifteen years of age and will reach reproductive age within a few years. Male-female ratios show that the proportion of immigrant women in Spain is high and in some regions higher than that of immigrant men. For example, among African immigrants the male-female ratio is 118, among Asians 101, and among Latin Americans 85 (Marrodán and Prado 1994).

In a report prepared in the early 1990s (Marrodán et al. 1991b), we estimated that there were about 200,000 migrant women from developing countries and Eastern Europe in Spain, and only one fourth of them had obtained legal residence. The growing immigration in Spain in the last five years and the demographic characteristics described above justify a study of reproductive and family models of these migrant populations. A study of this nature is also important for improving the quality of public health services for immigrants in Spain. Health providers should take into consideration the needs of different immigrant groups who frequently do not have the same coverage as the native population.

Because of the ages of most migrant women, their most important health needs are related to reproduction and family planning. Obstetric-gynecological issues include physiological as well as cultural dimensions, and reproductive behavior and health problems derived from it are to some extent influenced by the educational and cultural backgrounds of migrants. In order to resolve the health needs of migrant women, health policies have to take into account the social, economic, and cultural characteristics of migrants who, as will be shown, are very different. Policy makers run the risk of grouping all foreign-born persons—particularly all those from developing countries—under a single label of migrants, regardless of their culture, social background, and reasons for migration. Policies that ignore this diversity will have, at best, a limited impact.

It is not easy to obtain information regarding reproductive behavior because of the intimacy of sexual behavior. This is even more difficult in the case of migrants, who find themselves frequently in a hostile environment. In spite of these difficulties and based on our positive previous research experiences (Marrodán et al. 1991a, Prado et al. 1991), in 1992 we decided to begin a research project to fill the existing vacuum of information on reproductive behavior of migrant women in Spain.

The project examined the sociocultural conditions before and after migration, health behavior, and clinical histories of respondents, with particular emphasis on gynecological aspects. We also studied reproductive behavior and family planning and variations caused by migration. The project employed anthropometric measures that were used to measure the nutritional status and physical conditions of migrant women. Finally, we measured dietary changes introduced by migration, and the women's psychological adaptation to the receiving society. All facets of the fieldwork were carried out by the authors, and the anthropometric measures followed the I.B.P. norms (Weiner and Lourie 1991).

Respondents were contacted at Red Cross and public health centers, at refugee centers, and at NGOs that assist immigrants. The interviews, anthropometric measures, and blood tests took place in the same locations where respondents were contacted, but the medical consultations took place at the health centers. The interviews were conducted in Spanish, English, and French by members of the team. In the case of immigrants who did not know any of these languages, the researchers were assisted by friends or relatives of the respondents, who translated the questions and the answers.

Legal and Socioeconomic Status of Migrant Women

For purposes of the present paper we have grouped respondents by place of origin: Latin America Southern Cone (Argentina, Chile, and Uruguay), Latin America (rest), Sub-Saharan Africa, Middle East, Maghreb, and Eastern Europe. Table 8.1 shows respondents by region of origin and by legal status in Spain. The table shows that less than a quarter have obtained legal residence or citizenship. This is not the place to discuss the meaning of legal residence in Spain, but it should be noted that often legal residence—particularly for labor immigrants—is tied to employment: if at the time of renewal of the visa the migrant does not have an employer, he or she loses the right to remain in the country. About 30 percent of our respondents are refugees, a status that does not allow them to be lawfully employed, and 13 percent are illegal migrants. The higher percentages of illegality are found among Latin Americans (except those from the Southern Cone), women from the Maghreb, and those from Sub-Saharan Africa. Refugees are primarily women from Eastern Europe, the Middle East, and Sub-Saharan Africa.

Table 8.2 presents the educational levels of the groups and reveals that there are profound educational differences among women migrants. At

Table 8.1. Legal Status of Immigrant Women, by Region of Origin, 1994 (percentages)

Status	Southern Cone	Latin America (rest)	Sub-Saharan Africa	Middle East	Eastern Europe	Maghreb	*Total*
Illegal	4	21	16	2	2	20	13
Being processed	42	38	22	37	22	23	33
Refugee or exiled	2	23	47	51	61	20	30
Legal residence	44	16	13	10	12	31	20
Citizen	7	2	3	0	2	6	3
Total	99	100	101	100	99	100	99
n	(45)	(151)	(32)	(41)	(41)	(35)	(345)

Table 8.2. Educational Levels of Immigrant Women, by Region
of Origin, 1994 (percentages)

Educational Level	Southern Cone	Latin America (rest)	Sub-Saharan Africa	Middle East	Eastern Europe	Maghreb	Total
Illiterate	0	1	9	7	5	29	6
Primary	7	18	16	29	17	46	20
Intermediate	42	45	66	22	22	11	38
High-school diploma	24	9	6	17	15	6	12
University	27	27	3	24	42	9	24
Total	100	100	100	99	101	101	100
n	(45)	(152)	(32)	(41)	(41)	(35)	(346)

one end of the spectrum Maghrebian women, most of whom are from Morocco, have the highest levels of illiteracy (29 percent), and at the other end, migrants from the Southern Cone have the lowest. Women from Eastern Europe hold the largest number of university degrees, in contrast with women from Sub-Saharan countries and from the Maghreb.

Their condition as migrants and the precariousness of their legal status force many women to work in occupations well below those they could aspire to given their training. Only 6 percent of Eastern European and 4 percent of Southern Cone women are able to obtain work positions that are similar in status to those which they had before they migrated to Spain.

Income corresponds to the type of employment obtained, which, as indicated above, tends to be low for migrant women. Work in the informal sector/underground economy and underemployment are common. In general, it can be said that among those migrants who are employed the average income is slightly below the interprofessional minimum salary. It is for this reason that only a small percentage of migrant women have their own housing, while the majority share a flat with other persons or families in conditions that can best be described as overcrowded. It is not unusual for migrants to stay for a few months upon arrival in Spain in special housing facilities for migrants provided by the government or by nonprofit humanitarian associations.

Reproductive Characteristics and Behavior

Reproductive characteristics of migrant women are presented in table 8.3. Age at menarche was estimated by the retrospective method—asking the respondents to recall their age at the time of the event (correction factor 0.5). The validity of this method has been widely corroborated. There are statistically significant variations ($p < 0.01$) by geographical areas of the age at which first menstruation took place. As an average, first menstruation for women from the Southern Cone took place at 12.88 years of age, while for Sub-Saharan women it was at 14.37. There were also statistically significant differences ($p < 0.05$) between the former and women from the Middle East and Maghreb whose menarcheal age was 13.20. Traditionally, menarcheal age has been considered to be a measurement of social and nutritional status as well as of quality of life (Tanner 1990), and consequently we can affirm that immigrant women in Spain from the Middle East, Maghreb, and the Sub-Saharan region have a clear socioeconomic disadvantage.

Table 8.3 also shows that women who have an earlier menarcheal age (women from the Southern Cone and Eastern Europe) tend to marry at an older age, while those with a late menarcheal age (Sub-Saharan women) tend to marry earlier.

There are also major differences among regions regarding the number of children. About 20 percent of Southern Cone married women have no children, while there were no married women without children from the Maghreb and Middle East. Socioeconomic and cultural differences probably explain the variations. On the other hand, different cultures react differently to women who have never been married and have children. In our sample, there are more unmarried women with children from the Southern Cone and from Eastern Europe than in the other groups. About 6 percent of Sub-Saharan women had one or more children out of wedlock but two thirds of them got married later on. It is well known that unmarried women with children do not have a negative image in all societies; religion and culture play an important role in the way single mothers are perceived by their own societies. In some countries, such as Equatorial Guyana, women can get married more easily after they have a child, as this is a way to demonstrate that they are not sterile (Sainz de la Maza and González Kirchner 1991).

There are also important variations in family size, as can be observed in table 8.3. As could be expected, women from more developed countries

Table 8.3. Reproductive Cycle and Family Characteristics of Immigrant Women, by Region of Origin, 1994

	South-ern Cone	SD	Latin America (rest)	SD
Menarcheal age	12.9	0.86	13.1	1.03
Age at marriage	23.6	6.12	22.7	3.44
Menarche-marriage distance	10.7	3.99	9.4	3.35
First birth after marriage (months)	13.6	8.08	17.3	9.21
First–second birth (months)	30.8	10.4	31.0	9.0
Second–third birth (months)	40.2	12.0	28.4	10.7
Third–fourth birth (months)	37.0	13.2	29.9	14.4
Number of children	1.3	1.03	2.6	1.45
Breast-feeding (months)	4.3	3.5	8.5	3.09
Postpartum amenorrhea	3.0	3.68	7.8	6.8
Single mothers (%)	12.5	—	7.5	—
Married without children (%)	19.6	—	13.0	—
Users of birth control (%)	67.0	—	47.0	—
Fetal losses per woman	0.2	—	0.3	—

(Southern Cone and Eastern Europe) have the smaller number of children. We found the expected correlation between family size and use of birth control. In the case of Sub-Saharan migrant women, it should be noted that those who use birth control began to use it in Spain. There are profound differences in breast-feeding practices, which also have birth

Sub-Saharan Africa	SD	Middle East/ Maghreb	SD	Eastern Europe	SD
14.4	1.11	13.2	1.14	12.9	0.94
20.7	3.2	21.7	3.48	23.7	5.4
6.7	5.5	8.4	4.88	10.6	2.71
28.4	6.94	22.2	9.45	16.9	9.59
29.9	8.48	29.4	14.24	27.5	13.8
24.0	17.5	27.1	8.36	41.0	16.1
30.3	13.6	45.6	15.23	46.0	17.3
2.9	0.68	2.8	0.53	1.6	0.42
12.8	3.2	14.7	5.69	5.1	3.63
10.4	3.15	9.4	4.95	4.4	2.8
6.0	—	0.0	—	13.0	—
6.0	—	0.0	—	15.0	—
20.0	—	48.1	—	54.5	—
0.07	—	0.2	—	0.6	—

control effects. Middle Eastern, Maghrebian, and Sub-Saharan women breast-feed their children for extensive periods, almost fifteen and thirteen months respectively. Attitudes toward abortion are quite different. Migrant women from all groups except from the Southern Cone and Eastern Europe declared all abortions to be spontaneous, but among these two groups 25 and 58 percent respectively of the abortions were induced. The highest rate of abortions is among Eastern European women, with 0.6 fetal losses per woman.

Child spacing varies by migrant groups. As noted earlier, women from the Sub-Saharan region, from the Maghreb, and from the Middle East tend to marry earlier than women from the other groups and have a shorter menarche–marriage period. These women also wait longer after marrying to have the first child (28.4 and 22.2 months respectively). It is possible that the prolonged waiting period is the result of physiological immaturity rather than a personal decision to postpone the first pregnancy. Our analysis of time elapsed between subsequent pregnancies is very limited because in our sample there are very few parities above the third one. Nevertheless, we can detect a tendency to maintain a more constant reproductive rhythm among all groups except those from the Southern Cone and Eastern Europe, who seem to have a shorter reproductive period, with larger time intervals between parities. In general, it can be suggested that the larger the number of children, the more constant the reproductive rhythm.

From the foregoing analysis we can conclude that migrant women in Spain present different reproductive models that are in fact quite contrasting and reflect the cultures and levels of development of countries of origin. On the one hand, there is the model followed by Eastern European and Southern Cone migrants, characterized by a relatively early menarcheal age, marriage after twenty-three years of age, menarche–marriage intervals of more than ten years, small family size (an average of one or two children), and breast-feeding periods of less than six months. The second model is the one followed by the rest of Latin American, Sub-Saharan, Maghrebian, and Middle Eastern migrant women. This model is characterized by later menarcheal age, earlier marriage (before twenty-two years of age), menarche–marriage intervals of less than nine years, larger family size, and breast-feeding periods of more than eight months.

Reproductive health and family planning patterns are also very different among the different migrant groups. Women from the Southern Cone and Eastern Europe are totally familiarized with effective birth control methods and get regular medical and gynecological checkups. On the other hand, women from less developed countries or more traditional cultures learn for the first time about birth control in Spain. In their countries of origin, these women did not have access to medical and birth control services, or birth control was not accepted culturally. With some frequency, migrant women begin to practice new reproductive be-

Table 8.4. Symptoms of Menstrual Syndromes, Immigrant
Women, by Region of Origin, 1994 (percentages)

Symptoms	Eastern Europe	Southern Cone	Latin America (rest)	Middle East/ Maghreb	Sub-Saharan Africa
Depression	23	23	5	13	6
Breast tenderness	46	35	32	32	20
Skin alterations	23	10	10	0	0
Headaches	19	15	19	17	6
Edema	0	0	2	13	20
Backaches	18	8	5	9	0
Kidney aches	41	3	5	16	7
Dysmenorrhea	5	50	32	42	53
Amenorrhea	5	8	7	10	19
Irregular cycles	18	30	27	13	27
Bleeding days	4.4 +/− 1.4	4.7 +/− 2.0	4.1 +/− 2.6	4.8 +/− 2.8	5.1 +/− 2.3

haviors in Spain while maintaining their own cultural identity. The process of adaptation to the receiving society and its culture varies according to the migrant's age, her level of education, and the culture of her country of origin.

Table 8.4 shows the menstrual syndrome characteristics of the different migrant groups. Frequently, symptoms such as amenorrhea and irregularities are manifestations of difficulties and psychological problems, often caused by adverse social conditions. Amenorrhea (excluding during pregnancy and postpartum) is more frequent among Sub-Saharan, North African, and Middle Eastern migrants. Cycle irregularities are highest among Latin American, North African, and Middle Eastern migrants, but there are no significant differences by groups for days of bleeding. On the other hand, there are notable differences in the percentage of women who suffer dysmenorrhea. It should be noted that migrants with the largest number of children—Latin American (except from the Southern Cone), Middle Eastern, and Maghrebian migrants—are the ones with the less frequent dysmenorrhea.

As can be seen in table 8.4, there are significant differences among migrant groups regarding depression, breast tenderness, skin alterations, headaches, edemas, backaches, and kidney aches. All of these could also be signs of psychological disorders caused by harsh living conditions, physical trauma experienced in the past (torture, political persecution, etc.), or the difficulties of living in a foreign culture (family separation, discrimination, and racism). The incidence of depression is particularly high among Eastern European and Southern Cone migrants. A relatively large percentage of migrants from Eastern Europe also exhibit breast pains, skin alterations, backaches, and kidney aches. In contrast, Sub-Saharan migrants show the lowest percentage of symptoms, with the exception of edemas. The next step in our research is to find possible explanations for these differences and the possible role played by migration itself. For example, conditions caused by the migration (family separation, living conditions), or migration status (illegality), may be more important variables than region of origin in explaining differences in some of the above syndromes. Similarly, political refugees who were exposed to trauma at home may exhibit more severe symptoms of depression than labor migrants. In other words, there could be other variables in addition to country of origin or culture that explain the frequency and severity of some of the symptoms. Health providers should be aware of the possible origin of the symptoms in order to offer adequate therapeutic regimens and make appropriate referrals to social workers or clinical psychologists.

Our survey did not quantify health service needs and demands, but it should be mentioned that we noted a large demand for health services among immigrant women in Spain. The small number of health centers in Spain that provide care to immigrants not covered by the social security system (under which all natives and entitled immigrants receive free care; see Ugalde in this volume) is suggestive of an unsatisfied demand among some immigrants. The center in Majadahonda near Madrid, with which our research team collaborates, is a good case in point. Specifically, the demand for gynecological services in this center is very high. In spite of the assistance provided by the municipality and by many volunteer physicians, there continues to be an unmet demand. In sum, the health needs of many migrants are not adequately covered at present in Spain, and a solution must be found to provide comprehensive and regular health care to these new Spaniards.

References

Bolzman, C. 1993. "La place des femmes dans une emigration politique: L'example de l'exile chilien vers la Suisse." In Y. Preiswerk and J. Vallet, eds.,

Vers un ailleurs prometteur . . . L'emigration: Une response universalle a une situation de crise. Paris: Presses Universitaires de France, pp. 184–197.

Chapman, J. 1991. "Factors in Nineteenth-Century Swiss Emigration to the United States." Paper presented at the Colloque Pluridisciplinaire "L'emigration: Une response universalle a une situation de crise?" June 1991, Le Chable, Switzerland.

David, I. 1990. "Situación de las mujeres iberoamericanas en España." In *Las mujeres en América Latina: Una aproximación necesaria.* Barcelona: Ediciones Fundación CIPIE and Department of Sociology, Autonomous University of Barcelona.

Marrodán, M. D., I. David, C. Sancho, M. C. Santamarta, and A. Relaño. 1991a. *Mujeres del tercer mundo en España: Modelo migratorio y caracterización sociodemográfica.* Madrid: Ediciones Fundación CIPIE.

Marrodán, M. D., A. Sánchez-Andrés, E. M. Pérez de Landazabal, C. Prado, R. Rivero, A. H. Nielsen, and R. Martínez. 1991b. "La mujer inmigrante en España: Caracterización epidemiológica y factores de riesgo." In M. C. Botella et al., eds., *Nuevas perspectivas en antropología.* Granada: Diputación Provincial de Granada, pp. 511–520.

Marrodán, M. D., and C. Prado, eds., 1994. *Las migraciones: Su repercusión en la sociedad y en la biología de las poblaciones humanas.* Madrid: Editorial de la Universidad Autónoma de Madrid.

Prado, C., R. Rivero, E. Pérez de Landazabal, R. Martínez, M. D. Marrodán, A. H. Nielsen, and A. Sánchez. 1991. "La mujer inmigrante en España." In M. C. Botella et al., eds., *Nuevas perspectivas en antropología.* Granada: Diputación Provincial de Granada, pp. 783–789.

Sainz de la Maza, M., and J. P. González Kirchner. 1991. "Patrones de reproducción de la población de Bata (Guinea Ecuatorial)." In M. C. Botella et al., eds., *Nuevas perspectivas en antropología.* Granada: Diputación Provincial de Granada, pp. 883–892.

Tanner, J. M. 1990. "Growth as a Mirror of Conditions in Society." In G. W. Lindgren, ed., *Growth as a Mirror of Conditions in Society.* Stockholm: Stockholm Institute of Education Press, pp. 9–48.

Tapinos, G. P. 1990. *Inmigration féminine et statut des femmes étrangeres en France.* Paris: Institut National d'Etudes Demographiques.

Weiner, S. J., and J. A. Lourie. 1981. *Practical Human Biology.* London: Academic Press.

Zeverín, D. 1985. "La joven mujer inmigrante." A report prepared for the Red Cross. Cruz Roja de la Juventud, Madrid.

9

Psychopathology of Immigrants and Cross-Cultural Therapy

Antoine Gailly and Redouane Ben Driss

Causes of Mental Disorders

Much research has been done on migration and mental disorders. It is difficult, however, to compare the results of these studies because of sociodemographic differences and differences in diagnostic measures. The data are also gathered in different situations (hospitals, centers for mental health, etc.) so that the samples of subjects studied are not homogeneous. Theory building from single or case studies is difficult also because the situation of immigrants varies from one host country to another depending on historical and legislative differences between those countries. In addition, migration is a rather dynamic, not static, process and most of the data are the result of cross-sectional rather than longitudinal studies. Therefore, the results of these studies can hardly be compared, but some general implications can be drawn (for a literature survey, see Westermeyer 1989a, 1989b).

There are two theories that relate mental disorders and migration. According to premigratory theory, migration merely triggers the onset of the mental disorder. Some immigrants are predisposed to develop a mental disorder, and the migration stress elicits the illness. A second theory is that migration produces chronic cumulative stress that might cause mental disorders. This implies that the incidence of mental disorders increases depending on the period of time spent in the host country. According to this theory, the second generation of immigrants, those born in the host country, would be more vulnerable, which means that among this group the prevalence of delinquency and mental disorders increases. Both theories raise the question of whether migration is either a direct or an indirect cause of mental disorders.

Two main categories of causes related to migration that influence the prevalence of mental disorders can be distinguished. The first one is situated in the premigration period, and the second refers to the migratory background.

PREMIGRATORY FACTORS

The decision to migrate and the social adaptation in the host country are clearly influenced by the immigrant's personality, with the exception of paranoid and schizoid personalities, which present a different process. Some personality types that are considered marginal in a traditional society can become well-adapted in a Western society and vice versa.

Immigrants who expect to become rich and who idealize their future in the host country are more likely to develop mental disorders. Immigrants often arrive with high hopes of a better life and of forgetting their painful past. But sometimes the socioeconomic living conditions in the host country turn out to be difficult. Adaptation may be easier and stress less intense if the immigrant has some knowledge about the host country's culture and language.

FACTORS RELATED TO THE MIGRATORY BACKGROUND

The cultural differences between the home society and the host society can influence the prevalence of mental disorders among immigrants. The greater the cultural disparities, the higher the risk of morbidity.

Ethnic enclaves can favor the immigrant's adaptation to the host society, but they can also make integration all the more difficult, given the self-contained character of the enclaves. Relations both within and outside the group play an important role in the prevalence of psychopathology. When the relationships within a group are bad, isolation caused by the self-containment of the group is a high risk factor.

The characteristics of the host society also might influence the appearance and the rate of mental disorders. The host society's attitude toward integration is very important. A number of studies have shown that, in the short term, the "melting pot" principle implies psychological problems for the immigrant. In the long term, however, this situation may bring psychosocial gratification.

The concept of integration and the desire to return home present some inconsistencies. Most immigrants, when they come to Belgium, nurture the dream of going back home. Men often realize their dream of retiring and spending most of their time in their home village, but children and grandchildren do not want to return. The return of the head of the household results in one-parent families. Women cannot leave their children behind even though they also would like to return. Leaving their children seems much more difficult than did leaving their parental home many years before. Some governments, such as those of Germany, the Netherlands, and Belgium, favor a policy of integration through education, housing, and equality of opportunity. These governments want the immigrants to adapt to the host society, but at the same time they want immigrants to preserve their own culture in order to keep open the possibility of remigration (which is supported by the return allowance, a sum of money paid by the government to immigrants who decide to go back permanently to their home country).

Immigrants' education and occupations can have different effects on their postmigratory integration. Adaptation will become easier if the immigrants' education is recognized in the host society. However, if the immigrants expect too much from this recognition, they will be all the more disappointed because their education makes them more sensitive to differences. Studies have shown that, compared with older immigrants, those of the younger generation quite rapidly recover the social and professional status they had before emigration. On the other hand, adolescent immigrants seem to give up studying and immediately enter the labor force in the host country. Moreover, mood disorders and anxiety disorders seem to be related to education: difficulties in social adaptation can result from a low level of education. These difficulties are reflected in unemployment, social isolation, and a lack of knowledge of the host country's language. Age is also significant: immigrants asking for psychiatric care are between their late adolescence and their forties. This is not surprising as psychiatric disorders, such as schizoparanoia or anxiety disorders, usually occur between the ages of twenty and thirty.

We also must mention that the population of elderly immigrants in Europe is still very small. Therefore, little is known about the specific problems aging immigrants might experience in the future. Some trends, however, are already clear. Migration is a process of mobility not only in space but also in time. Elderly persons live in a different culture than the one into which they were born. In this sense elderly people live a double migration, and their problems are those faced by elderly people of any ethnic culture combined with the problems of being a foreigner. This perspective enables us to understand some conflicts between youngsters, parents, and grandparents as intergenerational conflicts. Immigrants displace these conflicts, often onto external factors. For example, parents in the home countries ascribe the cause of their immigrant children's re-fusal of arranged marriages to the U.S.-produced television series their children watch. In Belgium many older immigrants say that their children are affected by Belgian society.

Sex differences do not seem to be a significant factor in explaining mental disorders among immigrants. Women tend to express more chronic anxiety, whereas men show more acute anxiety. A more thorough statistical analysis, however, shows a correlation between sex, psychological complaints, unemployment, and the period of immigration. This correlation can be explained by the fact that women stick to their traditional way of life and that men lose their jobs and their social status following emigration. When men then become more integrated in the host society by means of their occupational activities, the incidence of mental disorders among male immigrants decreases, which is not the case for female immigrants.

EPIDEMIOLOGICAL ASPECTS

Pathological symptoms appearing shortly after migration are to be found among immigrants who are older than the group average and who have a lower education and a rather limited knowledge of the host country's language, and also among unemployed female immigrants. Problems of alcohol and drug abuse, delinquency, and feelings of failure as well as somatoform disorders and neurosis are more prevalent among men.

The incidence of major mental disorders such as psychoses and anxiety disorders increases among immigrants with a higher than average level of education. Immigrants suffering from these disorders usually are younger, are unemployed, and have a good knowledge of the host country's language.

In general, immigrants who are joined by their family and whose children are born in the host country often suffer from relational problems. These problems may lead to delinquency, drug or alcohol addiction, and academic failure. Because of language problems, the child becomes the parent's interpreter and thus takes over part of his or her parent's social status. At the same time, the authority of the father is at stake, and the traditional roles and values, as well as family dynamics, change. Unemployment makes these problems even worse. Economic crises make the labor market much more selective, and immigrants turn out to be the victims of a double discrimination: not only as foreigners but also as unskilled workers.

Children of immigrant parents often have problems at school and drop out after primary school. During childhood, girls generally have less problems keeping up than boys of the same age. Their situation, however, becomes more difficult once they reach adolescence, when they have to behave in a more traditional way that values being married to a "pure" boy from the country of origin and becoming a good spouse and house-wife. Studying is often equated with becoming European.

In Belgium, as in most West European countries, there is a need for nationwide or regional epidemiological studies of immigrants, political refugees, and asylum seekers. Studies about their health and medical needs as well as their knowledge of and attitudes toward health, illness, and care are limited to private medical practices.

The studies cover various topics ranging from methodological novelties, health status, preventive behavior, risky habits, primary health care visits, intake of medicines, medical views, and conceptions of how the Belgian health system functions. Over the last ten years the researchers' focus of attention has moved beyond case reporting and the descriptive work that set out to give a cultural explanation for the way ethnic minorities deal with health problems. The main achievements are methodological development, prenatal care work, subjective and objective health status work, an analysis of the medical demands on the general practitioner, psychosomatic problems, and the work on assessing the quality of care (Van de Mieroop, Peeters, and De Muynck 1989, De Muynck and Peeters 1994). In the literature frequent mention is made of more psychological disturbances (namely, mental disorders) among Turks in comparison with the indigenous population. This cannot, however, be inferred from the level of use of medical services, as immigrants are admitted in even fewer numbers than are autochthonous residents to mental homes. The Centers for Mental Health, part of the secondary care sector, also have very few immigrants among their clientele. Nonetheless, the primary care sector complains that it is not able to refer immigrants with psychological problems. In addition, alleged language problems and cultural differences—such as "the client can't speak the language well enough" or "the client belongs to a different culture" or even "the client hovers between two cultures"—encountered by the social worker but also by the person requesting treatment can affect the transference and feedback to such an extent that a therapeutic process becomes very difficult if not impossible. So immigrants are looked upon, a priori, as clients who cannot be helped. In spite of communication and other problems, both public services and individual providers of care, apart from a few exceptions, appear to be little concerned about improving the communication with immigrant patients in order to improve the quality of care provided or about involving immigrants in the discussion of the provision of medical care (Peeters, Gailly, and De Muynck 1994).

Some other general trends in the literature (Gailly 1988) indicate that the incidence of postmigratory mental disorders does not seem to increase, that schizophrenia and depression seem to be overdiagnosed among immigrants, and that some psychological problems are rather expressed in mood and anxiety disorders and in particular symptoms, including a tendency toward somatization.

From our research (Gailly 1985, 1988, 1991, 1997; Devisch and Gailly 1985; Gailly and Devisch 1984; Gailly, Devisch, and Corveleyn 1985) it seems clear that somatization disorders result from chronic stress linked to relational problems within the extended family. There is no evidence that migration factors directly cause somatization disorders. Migration seems to have only an indirect effect by altering the intrafamilial relations. Because of unemployment, Turkish men no longer have an identity via their occupation. This means that they no longer can claim an identity in terms of participation in Western society. While they used to be "miners," now they are "Muslims." Lack of participation in the Western society enhances the feeling of belonging to the ethnic group, and immigrant societies become more and more self-contained. Immigrants try to preserve their own culture, and social control is very strong. The cultural tradition and religion they claim and use as ethnic markers, however, often differ a great deal from what can be found in their home villages. They do not refer to their country as it is today but to the country they left behind and as they perceive it from the perspective of the immigrant. The result is that migrant men are thrown back on their own society and end up in a vacuum, where the fall is often cushioned by a "fun and games" economy (frequenting public houses, gambling, prostitution, drinking, dating Eastern European women, and so on).

Women look upon this kind of husband as a "child," as an adolescent with "a fool's blood," as a good-for-nothing. The children may acquire a very negative image of their father that influences their perspective on the future and their motivation (Gailly 1991, Phalet 1993). In the Turkish culture, the public world is seen as the man's space, while indoors the mother represents the positively valorized father to the children. In immigration studies we refer to a physical and symbolic "absent father figure," so in the upbringing of the children this gives rise to an absence of fixed rules and laws. Women have to take on simultaneously the male as well as the female roles, which results in a chronically high level of stress.

Problems in Cross-Cultural Therapy

When confronted with suffering, people rely on scientific and medical as well as ethnomedical and ethnopsychiatric systems (the latter often called traditional healing systems) in order to give meaning to, and to get help for, diseases. "Cross-cultural" therapy occurs when the care provider and the client belong to different cultures. Differences in cultural references may interfere with the therapeutic process and may lead to misunderstandings (Leman and Gailly 1991). The presence of ethnic minorities in need of mental health care leads us to examine the difficulties implied in cross-cultural therapies, the analyses of patients' needs, and the cultural meaning of mental disorders.

LANGUAGE PROBLEMS AND CULTURAL DIFFERENCES

When the care provider and the client do not speak a common language, obviously there are communication problems. Resorting to interpreters from the patient's ethnic community may prevent some complaints from being expressed, especially when the interpreter belongs to the family of the client. When the client expresses family or intimate problems, the interpreter might censor them and/or give standard answers. The use of interpreters also changes the therapeutic context. The care provider–client dyadic relationship becomes a threesome with all the complications this entails: changes in roles and different trust issues, to name two. Even if the care provider and the client do speak a common language, cultural codes of complaints and diagnoses are not always understood.

Care providers and clients may consciously or unconsciously use language problems and cultural differences to account for the difficulties in cross-cultural situations. When the care provider speaks the client's language, he or she is perceived as belonging to the client's community and thus will likely elicit high expectations and a highly positive transference. This changes drastically when the client's expectations are not met. After all, the care provider will be perceived as belonging to another culture, and, being a stranger, he or she is unable to understand the client's problem. The care provider might even be considered a racist. These processes of transference can also occur when the care provider and the client are members of the same ethnic group, because the client can think that the provider no longer belongs to the client's group because he or she has become educated. Under these conditions therapy cannot start because neither party is able to meet the other's expectations.

PROBLEMS IN THERAPY

When therapy does start, other problems may arise. With a lack of anthropological information, the care provider might interpret the cultural material the client presents to be of a psychological nature. The fact that one claims to be possessed by a spirit, however, does not necessarily mean that one is psychotic. Moreover, if the care provider tries to obtain cultural information within the context of therapy, the client becomes an anthropological informant. This is not the reason the client came to see the care provider, and the client receives no information that he or she did not already know. It is very difficult to change the client's position of informant because this situation favors and intensifies his or her cultural defense mechanisms, and the care provider finds herself or himself listening to a cultural presentation, which constitutes resistance to a therapeutic approach (Devereux 1977). Therefore, we would maintain that the ethnopsychiatric approach and the psychotherapeutic approach are contradictory. The care provider must be able to go beyond cultural speech because the immigrant client should be not a cultural but rather a psychological informant.

STAGES OF REJECTION

In Belgium, clients are often referred to psychotherapists by general practitioners or by social workers with a letter cast in terms such as: "Dear colleague, I'm sending you a Turkish patient with psychological problems due to cultural differences, and he [or she] is in need of specialized treatment." This letter implies clearly that the patient has the problem and not that the care provider has a problem with the client. The client, however, interprets this as an admission of the care provider's incompetence, and the specialist has to build up a new therapeutic relationship. This is very difficult not only because of the created expectations but also because what stands out in the client's mind is the rejection of his or her personal involvement in the relationship with the previous care provider. Afraid of being rejected again, the patient may unconsciously cause this rejection as a way to restrain his or her own fears. Many immigrants, however, left their country in the first place because they felt rejected.

Conclusions

Therapists often consider linguistic problems and cultural differences as obstacles to cross-cultural therapy. Immigrant patients can also use these problems and differences, either consciously or unconsciously, to account for their weaknesses and transgressions and for their psychological problems. We can say that the differences between the therapists' and patients' cultural references present risks of misunderstanding and even nonunderstanding that can lead to unwanted effects in the therapeutic process.

This leads to the conclusion that as assistance to immigrants does not respond to their needs anymore, our approach must be reconsidered. We believe that in order to understand the immigrants' complaints and to be able to help them efficiently, existing clichés about linguistic, cultural, and socioeconomic barriers such as living and housing conditions, which are often considered to be the cause of migrants' somatoform disorders, must be reconsidered. Although these parameters are important, too often they are overestimated or applied from an ethnocentric point of view. This prompts the therapist to develop a sense of paternalism that in the long term leads to frustration and aggressiveness, which are difficult to overcome and which will be taken out on the patient. Sticking to clichés is also bound to lead to a kind of second-rate care provision that makes an intrapsychic approach unnecessary. We should therefore ask ourselves whether the immigrant's psychic world is given enough consideration and whether the image of it provided by therapists does not reinforce the negative opinions natives already have of immigrants.

References

De Muynck, A., and R. F. Peeters. 1994. "Hoe gezond zijn Ali en Fatma? Tien jaar wetenschappelijk onderzoek over gezondheid van en gezondheidszorg voor allochtonen in Vlaanderen (1984–1993): Een kritisch overzicht" [How Healthy Are Ali and Fatima? Ten Years of Scientific Research on Health and Health Care for Immigrants in Flanders (1984–1993): A Critical Review]. ESOC Publication no. 33. Antwerp: University of Antwerp.

Devereux, G. 1977. *Essais d'ethnopsychiatrie générale.* Paris: Gallimard.

Devisch, R., and A. Gailly. 1985. "Dertlesmek, The Sharing of Sorrow: A Therapeutic Self-Help Group among Turkish Women." *Psychiatria e Psicoterapia Analitica* 4: 133–152.

Gailly, A. 1983. *Een dorp in Turkije* [A Village in Turkey]. Brussels: Cultuur en Migratie.

———. 1985. "Life Recedes When Exchange Fails: Clinical Anthropology among Turkish Patients." *International Journal of Psychology* 20: 521–538.

———. 1988. *Psychische klachten bij Turken en hun benadering* [Psychological Complaints among Turks and Their Approach]. Brussels: Cultuur en Migratie.

————. 1991. "Time Perspective and Motivational Goals of Belgian and Turkish Adolescents in Belgium and of Turkish Adolescents in Turkey." Paper presented at the IACCP Congress, Liège.

————. 1997. "Turkish Immigrants in Belgium." In I. Al-Issa and M. Tousignant, eds., *Ethnicity, Immigration, and Psychopathology.* New York: Plenum Press.

Gailly, A., and R. Devisch. 1984. "No Son for My Stifling Husband: 'The Other' in Illness." *Analytic Psychotherapy and Psychopathology* 1: 151–163.

Gailly, A., R. Devisch, and J. Corveleyn. 1985. "'Etre' aux limites de sa condition: Analyse psychodynamique d'un cas de psychose hystérique en milieu Turc immigré en Belgique." In E. Jeddi, ed., *Psychose, famille et culture.* Paris: L'Harmattan.

Leman, J., and A. Gailly. 1991. *Thérapies interculturelles.* Brussels: De Boeck-Wesmael.

Peeters, R., A. Gailly, and A. De Muynck. 1994. "De geestelijke gezondheidszorg voor de allochtonen in Vlaanderen: Inventaris en aanzet tot evaluatie" [Mental Health Care for Immigrants in Flanders: Inventory and Start of an Evaluation]. *Diagnostiek-Wijzer* 1–2: 21–30.

Phalet, K. 1993. Culturele waarden en persoonlijke keuzen: Groepsloyaliteit en prestatiemotivatie bij Turkse en Belgische jongeren [Cultural Values and Personal Choices: Group Loyalty and Achievement Motivation among Turkish and Belgian Youth]. Doctoral diss., Department of Psychology, University of Leuven.

Van De Mieroop, E., R. Peeters, and A. De Muynck. 1989. "Hoe ziek zijn Ali en Fatma? Onderzoek naar ziekte en gezondheid van vreemdelingen in Vlaanderen en Brussel: Een stand van zaken" [How Sick Are Ali and Fatima? A Study of Sickness and Health of Foreigners in Flanders and Brussels: The Current Situation]. ESOC Publication no. 21. Antwerp: University of Antwerp.

Westermeyer, J. 1989a. *Psychiatric Care of Migrants :A Clinical Guide.* Washington, D.C.: American Psychiatric Press.

————. 1989b. *Mental Health for Refugees and Other Migrants.* Springfield, Ill.: Charles C. Thomas.

10

The Cultural Psychology of Immigration

Marcelo M. Suárez-Orozco

The United States is now in the midst of a major demographic transformation that will have profound implications for the future of U.S. democracy and cultural pluralism in the next millennium. It is estimated that by the year 2050 the population of the United States will be nearly 50 percent ethnic and racial minorities—largely made up of Hispanics or Latinos, African Americans, and Asian Americans.

The remaking of the U.S. nation is related to changes in immigration policies during the last few decades. After a period of relative neglect, immigration has once again recaptured public opinion with unprecedented force. The debate over immigration today centers on issues such as securing international borders against undocumented immigrants, the economics of immigration, the rights of legal immigrants to access a host of publicly funded services, issues relating to asylum, and issues of cultural identity among the children of immigrants.

The issue of immigration has come to evoke some profound anxieties about economic, social, and cultural formations at the *fin de siècle*. Unfortunately, much of the public debate about immigration seems to be governed by thalamic structures rather than by more refined neocortical principles. The immigration debate today is saturated with facile references to the economy, crime, and the cultural reshaping of the U.S. nation.

It is important to resist the impulse to view immigration through the old lenses of American exceptionalism. In the area of immigration, nearly all postindustrial democracies seem to be facing substantially similar issues. With well over one hundred million immigrants worldwide, immigration today is a global issue, arguably a central feature of a new transnational order. In virtually all major postindustrial democracies today few topics are as explosive as legal and undocumented immigration, the growing numbers of asylum seekers, and the adaptation problems of the children of immigrants (Suárez-Orozco 1996b).

131

On both sides of the Atlantic, there is a feeling that the world around is sinking and that the islands of privilege in Europe and North America simply cannot rescue all those who need rescuing. The language of the new immigration is the apocalyptic language of deluge: in ever-growing "waves," immigrants are said to be "flooding" the shores of the more developed world. Rickety boats carry immigrants and asylum seekers to the coasts of Florida or New York just as they do to the coasts of Mediterranean Europe.

Strikingly, the new immigration is engendering remarkable similarities in a number of otherwise distinct countries—in most of Western Europe, throughout the United States, and now even in Japan. Countries that in the recent past welcomed and indeed actively recruited immigrant laborers, such as Belgium and France, are now in a decidedly anti-immigrant mood. Countries that until recently generously granted refuge, such as Germany, are now severely restricting the access of asylum seekers (Cornelius, Martin, and Hollifield 1994).

There is increasing evidence that on both sides of the Atlantic public opinion has rapidly turned against legal and undocumented immigration. Surveys in Brussels suggest that a majority of Flemish voters—up to 70 percent according to some studies—would like to see the immigrants go back home (Suárez-Orozco 1994). Likewise in the United States, polls continue to suggest that many citizens feel that immigration has become harmful to the country (Espenshade and Hempstead 1996).

The debate over immigration and ethnicity has taken a decidedly post-utopian twist. Long-privileged notions of immigrant "assimilation," "acculturation," and multiethnic harmony have been overwhelmed by neonativistic anxieties. In France, the once reigning notion that French culture could assimilate all immigrant groups has been guillotined. France today routinely sends back undocumented immigrants and asylum seekers to North Africa and Eastern Europe.

In neighboring Flanders, Belgium, voters sent political shock waves through the European landscape by electing a member of the neo-Nazi Vlaams Blok mayor of the elegant city of Antwerp. The Vlaams Blok's rather narrow political platform is well captured in its slogan, "Our people first, seal our borders, send the immigrants home." Likewise in Austria the leader of the far right Freedom Party, Joerg Haider, recently announced his intention to make immigration a key theme of the next electoral campaign. Indeed, immigration issues—and denying the Holocaust—have become the *cause célèbre* of Europe's far right groups.

On November 8, 1994, California voters overwhelmingly approved Proposition 187, known as the "Save our State" initiative, claiming:

> [the People of California] have suffered and are suffering economic hardship caused by the presence of illegal aliens in this state.
> That they have suffered and are suffering personal injury and damage caused by the criminal conduct of illegal aliens in this state.
> That they have a right to the protection of their government from any person or persons entering this country unlawfully.
> Therefore, the people of California declare their intention to provide for cooperation between their agencies of state and local government with the federal government, and to establish a system of required notification by and between such agencies to prevent illegal aliens in the United States from receiving benefits or public services in the State of California. (State of California 1994: 91)

Proposition 187 will, inter alia, exclude an estimated 300,000 undocumented immigrant children from public elementary and secondary educational institutions (Suárez-Orozco 1996a). The proposition's incendiary language and the unsettling debate around it (Feldman and McDonnell 1994, Feldman and Rainey 1994, McDonnell 1994, Mills 1994, Noble 1994) are revealing of the anxieties produced by immigration today.

Freud claimed that hysteria was the *malaise* of his civilization. As we approach the end of our century, hysteria over immigration has become one of the great discontents of our times. And as was the case in Freud's time, before we can treat *this* hysteria we must carefully consider the relative importance of fact and fantasy in its making. Slogans' claims that immigrants are driven into the wealthy postindustrial democracies by the magnet of the welfare state or to commit crimes may be catchy in political campaigns but are empirically dubious and intellectually dishonest.

What *are* the key relevant facts? First, a big part of today's immigration crisis in the postindustrial democracies is self-inflicted. Policies to recruit foreign workers to feed a voracious appetite for inexpensive labor has ignited—via transnational labor-recruiting networks, wage differentials, and family reunification—much of the recent undocumented population movement. For example, California's Governor Pete Wilson—who has masterfully manipulated anti-immigration sentiment with some political success—while a U.S. senator, promoted policies to bring foreign workers in response to the needs of California's big agribusiness. In 1986 Wilson and others from the California congressional delegation "held up passage of the Immigration Reform and Control Act until a provision was added to allow several hundred thousand immigrants into the country temporarily so that they could help harvest crops. Under the provision that eventually resulted, more than one million came to stay" (Brinkley 1994: 1).

A second fact is that even in the current ethos of anti-immigrant sentiment and high unemployment among native workers (in Western Europe unemployment rates are on average twice the U.S. rate), some market sectors continue to rely on "cheap" foreign workers to do what the Japanese now call the "3-K jobs" for the Japanese words for dirty, dangerous, and demanding jobs (Lydia Chávez 1994). On February 6, 1995, less than three months after passage of Proposition 187, the California attorney general, Don Lungren, among others, called for a *new* guest worker program to bring temporary agricultural workers to California.

Some immigration experts have argued that such guest worker programs are short-term fixes that produce long-term problems. Doris Meissner, the current Immigration and Naturalization commissioner, wisely noted that "the notion that a country can add workers to its labor force and not residents to its population is fundamentally flawed" (1992, p. 66). Furthermore, there are data that suggest that in certain sectors of the economy employers often prefer to hire the relatives and friends of immigrant workers they trust (see Waldinger 1994), thus generating new cycles of undocumented migration.

A third key fact is that recent immigration has been a by-product of stunning global economic and political transformations. Liberalization of developing economies—in much of Latin America engineered largely by U.S.-trained economists—has stimulated migratory patterns. In Mexico and Central America, a fierce pattern of competitive allocation of land between land-poor agriculturists and powerful transnational interests will continue to be a factor in immigration. Over the next two decades economic transformations related to NAFTA (North American Free Trade Agreement) will push perhaps two to three million Mexican farmers out of their lands.

Other transnational economic developments go hand-in-hand with today's immigration flows—be they legal or undocumented. The U.S. Treasury estimated that the December 1994 Mexican currency devaluation in which the peso's value dropped by 50 percent would increase undocumented immigration to the United States by as much as 30 percent

(Sanger 1995). Indeed, during February 1995 the number of undocumented immigrants apprehended in the southern border area jumped by 30 percent over the previous year's level.

In Western Europe there are isomorphic developments. Political upheaval in the former Soviet bloc and the spread of ethnonationalistic conflicts—such as in the former Yugoslavia—have accelerated population movements. European officials are keeping a watchful eye on developments in the Maghreb in general and in Algeria in particular. Many in France fear that the fall of the current Algerian government will produce a mass exodus. North-South differential demographic profiles (more than half the Maghreb's population is below the age of 25), high unemployment rates (about 50 percent in Algeria), and wage differentials (in 1992 the per capita GDP was $22,260 in France and $1,840 in Algeria) have remained powerful emigration "push" constants for much of this century. The U.S.–Mexico wage differential today is about six to one.

There is a common grammar to the transatlantic narratives that have come to dominate public debate over immigration. Broadly speaking, there are six distinct but related areas of overlapping concern. The first concern is a feeling on both sides of the Atlantic that there are simply too many new arrivals. Since 1990 Germany has processed over a million asylum cases. The United States now receives on average close to a million new documented immigrants and an estimated 200,000 to 400,000 new undocumented immigrants each year.

A second concern is rooted in the feeling that immigration controls—including employer sanctions—have largely failed to contain the numbers of undocumented immigrants and asylum seekers arriving year after year. The continued resistance of British authorities to turn over border controls to the European Union—per the Schengen agreement, which calls for a border-free Europe—reveals isomorphic concerns over "losing control" in the European landscape.

A third concern relates to trans-Atlantic anxieties about the economic consequences of immigration (Cornelius 1993, Linda Chávez 1994, Fierman 1994, Francese 1994, Glazer 1994, Miles 1994, Mills 1994, Rothstein 1994). In Europe those opposing immigration point to the rates of unemployment among immigrants—in some cases four times the rate of unemployment among native workers—and their reliance on the fabulously generous European social security system (Suárez-Orozco 1994). Likewise, in the United States some observers argue that the post-1965 wave of new immigration coincided with the expansion of the welfare state, creating irresistible temptations for immigrants to use—some say abuse—publicly funded services (Borjas 1994, Huddle 1993). A highly publicized study by the General Accounting Office noted that legal immigrants are almost twice as likely as citizens to receive cash welfare from a federal program. GOP legislators are now proposing to bar *legal* immigrants from many federally funded programs (Golden 1996).

The economic consequences of immigration are quite complex. Some economists such as Don Huddle (1993) and George Borjas (1994) argue that new immigrants are a burden to the economy. Other economists— on both sides of the Atlantic—have argued that immigrants on aggregate "produce" much more through taxation and other economic dynamics than they "consume" in public services (Passel 1994). Others have noted that in parts of Europe where fertility rates are below replacement levels, foreign workers will be key to future economic well-being.

Fourth, there is the incendiary charge that immigrants in general— and undocumented immigrants in particular—are contributing disproportionately to the problem of crime in host societies. The leader of Austria's Freedom Party recently announced, "The safety of our streets is directly linked to the problem of illegal aliens in Austria." In the United States fear of undocumented-immigrant crime was a key ingredient in the making of Proposition 187 (Suárez-Orozco 1996a). I must note that this highly charged indictment is not based on any empirically robust data. In fact, the only reasonable study of undocumented immigration and crime—conducted by Dan Wolf (1988)—suggests that undocumented immigrants in California are far more likely to be the victims of crime than the perpetrators.

The fifth concern relates to anxieties generated by the fact that the new arrivals are transforming the demographic landscape of various countries of immigration. In the United States today nearly 80 percent of all new arrivals are from Latin America, the Caribbean, and Asia. By contrast, in 1940 70 percent of all immigrants came from Europe. By early next century the United States will have the second largest number of Spanish speakers in the world. In Belgium today two thirds of all immigrants are from three countries: Morocco, Turkey, and Algeria. In France, 65 percent of all immigrants are from three North African countries: Algeria, Morocco, and Tunisia. In Germany 46 percent of all immigrants are from Turkey (Cornelius, Martin, and Hollifield 1994).

Sixth, there are anxieties that the children of the new south-to-north immigrants will not easily "assimilate" to the institutions of the various labor-importing democracies. Both sides of the Atlantic have seen a number of highly charged events capturing a clash in the symbolic space new immigrants and dominant societies are struggling to share. As Julia Kristeva, the grande dame of French psychoanalysis, put it, "France today is in the process of welcoming newcomers who do not give up their particularities" (1991: 194).

The recent battle in French schools—long proud of their secular tradition—over the right of Muslim girls to wear head scarves (*hidjab*) captured the cultural conflicts over forms of diversity and difference that are seen by many Europeans as highly problematic. Throughout Western Europe talk about "the problem of immigration" is intimately tied to anxieties about the future of Islam—particularly fundamentalism—in secular Europe. Likewise, on the eve of the recent California election, there was outrage among many voters when Latino students, some proudly displaying Mexican flags, took to the streets of San Francisco, Los Angeles, and San Diego to protest the campaign for Proposition 187. The flag incident—just like the head scarf incident—was interpreted by some as symptomatic of a studied refusal to "assimilate" among the children of the new immigrants.

Lost in these ever louder debates are the voices of the new arrivals themselves. Who *are* the new immigrants? What *do* they want? How *are* the children adapting to the process of upheaval and resettlement? Although we know quite a bit about immigrants, we know surprisingly little about immigration as a process. A significant weakness in the relevant literature, a problem we consciously set out to overcome in some of our recent research efforts, is that no study to date has systematically compared the experiences of would-be immigrants *before* migration with comparable samples of newly arrived immigrants and second-generation immigrants, along with a group of nonimmigrant members of the majority population.

In a recent fieldwork project Suárez-Orozco and Suárez-Orozco (1995) attempted to highlight how the family and school experiences of a sample of youths in the state of Guanajuato, a migrant-sending area of Mexico, differ from the experiences of comparable samples of newly arrived immigrants, second-generation U.S.-born Mexican Americans, and nonimmigrant, non-Latino "whites." Additionally, we attempted to provide a psychocultural theoretical framework for understanding these differences.

❖

By far the majority of Latinos in the United States are either immigrants or the children of migrants. Therefore, any serious consideration of the Latino condition must provide an understanding of how immigration shapes experience. In our view, immigration is an open-ended process that differentially affects the experiences of various generations (the migrant generation, the U.S.-born second generation, the third generation, etc.). Hence we are critical of theories of immigrant "assimilation" and "acculturation" that tend to offer premature closure to what is, in our estimation, an intergenerational dynamic process.

It has been recognized that the immigrant generation often arrives in a new land as pioneers, with a dream of making a better life for themselves as well as for their children. The objectives of the first-generation migrants anywhere in the world are relatively similar: get a job, save money, learn a new language, if possible offer an education to the children, and in general improve their lot in life. The obvious difficulties that most immigrants face may include language inadequacies, a general unfamiliarity with the customs and expectations of the new country, limited economic opportunities, poor housing conditions, discrimination, and more generally what psychologists term the "stresses of acculturation."

Despite these obstacles immigrants typically come to see their lot as having improved from what it was in their country of origin. There is a genre in the literature of immigration—recent examples of this work include, for example, Eva Hoffman's *Lost in Translation: A Life in a New Language* and Esmeralda Santiago's *Cuando era puertorriqueña*—when immigrants sit down to tell those left behind—in letters or in tape recordings—fantastic tales of life in the garden of Eden. What is striking about these narratives is the gap between the hardships in lived experiences of immigrants and their almost unreal depictions of their new lives when communicating with those left behind. Leo Festinger surely would have had a field day examining these documents in light of his theory of cognitive dissonance.

The Belgian anthropologist Eugeen Roosens has noted that because of a perception of relative improvement, particularly in their economic condition, immigrants may seem less concerned with the negative attitudes of the host country toward them, maintaining their group of origin as a point of reference (Roosens 1989: 132–134). Additionally, as George De Vos has argued, the immigrant generation commonly views its lot in a new environment not in terms of the ideals and expectations of the majority society but rather in terms of the ideals and expectations of the "old culture" (De Vos 1973). De Vos claimed that Japanese immigrants who relocated from the California internment camps to Chicago maintained social cohesiveness by keeping alive culturally constructed role expectations and ideals that helped inoculate them—particularly the children—from the degrading attitudes and expectations of the dominant culture.

This is part of a general orientation that we have termed "the immigrant's dual frame of reference" (Suárez-Orozco and Suárez-Orozco 1995). We have found that recently arrived immigrants constantly compare and contrast their new experiences in the host society with their previous experiences and expectations in the country of origin. Rogler, Cortés, and Malgady explore the psychosocial consequences of a generational discontinuity between the Mexico-born parents and their California-born children that relates to the immigrant's dual frame of reference. They write: "The selectivity of the migration stream from Mexico to California tends to create a psychologically robust first-generation immigrant population who feels less deprived because migration has increased their standard of living; in contrast, the Mexican Americans born in the United States feel more deprivation because of their much higher but unrealized aspirations" (1991: 589). The children of immigrants indeed experience their lives in the new country differently than the immigrant generation. While immigrants often view their lot through the prism of relative gain, the second generation may under certain circumstances develop a sense of relative deprivation. Rather than seeing themselves as better off vis-à-vis the old country (as their parents did), many second-generation youths may view their situation as one of deprivation and marginality vis-à-vis the dominant culture (Horowitz 1983). Thus, members of the second generation often face many of the same difficulties as their parents *without* the perceived benefits. Ongoing discrimination and ethnic tension have an erosive effect, particularly in the more vulnerable children of immigrants.

The anthropologists George A. De Vos (1992) and John U. Ogbu (1974) have argued that the specific problems facing the children of immigrants and other minority groups are best seen in the context of the distinct psychosocial experiences of each group as it enters a dominant society. Ogbu (1974), under the influence of George De Vos (1973, 1992) and Robert LeVine (1966), developed a framework to systematically describe the special problems facing those minority groups that have been incorporated into a dominant society in an involuntary fashion—such as

African Americans through slavery or Native Americans and the original Mexican Americans through conquest. Furthermore, these groups have been subjected to what Ogbu calls a "job ceiling." Ogbu maintains that these groups were traditionally reserved the most undesirable menial jobs in the opportunity structure and could not rise above these positions regardless of effort, talent, motivation, or achievement.

George De Vos (1992) developed a cultural psychology of ethnic adaptation from his research among minorities in Japan and the United States. According to De Vos, in multiethnic societies characterized by patterned inequality and conflict, some ethnic and racial minorities often become the targets of what he calls "psychological disparagement." That is, they may be the target of symbolic violence, in which they are stereotyped as "innately inferior," "lazier," and "prone to crime."

Borrowing from various seminal works including Freud's *Civilization and Its Discontents* (1930), Dollard et al.'s work on frustration and aggression (1939), Kohut's work on narcissistic injury and rage (1972), Mitchell's work on the endangered self (1993), and Julia Kristeva's work on the distraught self (1991), I have argued that in times of upheaval immigrant and other minorities may be used for other psychosocial purposes. From my point of view, the construction of powerful landscapes of "Otherness"—discourses portraying immigrants as parasites and criminals taking our limited and diminishing resources, such as that found in the language of Proposition 187—is largely a projective mechanism serving primitive psychological functions in times of social malaise.

Heuristic models are relevant only when they can elucidate god in the details. Why, we may ask, are these anti-immigrant landscapes of Otherness so powerful in certain parts of the world today? The California experience may be paradigmatic.

California has recently endured unprecedented upheaval—in its economy, society, and nature. During much of the 1990s California has been facing huge post–Cold War losses in its military-industrial base and other key industries. There are deep anxieties about an ethos of diminishing expectations. A March 1995 UCLA poll found that 57 percent of Californians believed the state was on "the wrong track" (Sears 1995). (The real income of the median worker there has not increased in twenty years.) Their concerns were about crowded schools, violent crime, and stunning demographic changes—political minorities are fast becoming California's demographic majority. (Today Latinos represent over 25 percent of the California population.) Since the early 1990s California has suffered a number of devastating natural disasters, including floods, urban wild fires, and earthquakes at an estimated loss of over fifty billion dollars. The Rodney King affair was a social earthquake leaving much destruction and unresolved grief.

Psychologists of varied theoretical orientations have identified frustration, injury, and endangerment as a powerful context for aggression. It is in such a climate that those who are least like the dominant population—the new immigrants—have been singled out with a vengeance. My contention is that the anti-immigrant landscapes of Otherness that now saturate public discourse have emerged to contain overwhelming anxieties and focus righteous anger. I concur with Julia Kristeva when she writes that the idea of the malevolent Other or Stranger often "appears as a defense put up by a distraught self: it protects itself [by] the image of a malevolent double into which it expels the share of destruction it cannot contain" (Kristeva 1991: 183–184).

But this is only one side of the coin. There is a price in the economy of anger. The stranger, the Other, today's "malevolent immigrant," constructed to contain badness and focus anger, cannot fail but to activate powerful persecutorial fantasies. Melanie Klein's idea of the "bad object" is relevant here: the object constructed to contain badness becomes a powerfully charged persecutorial object (Klein and Riviere 1964). Hence, we come psychoculturally to close the circle of fear and hatred. The immigrant "Other" charged with "badness" is now experienced as persecutorial criminal or parasite that must be expelled.

Powerful envy fantasies are also critical ingredients in the organization of irrational fears. Consider the ferocity of the language presented to California voters (reading from the ballot material in support of Proposition 187): "Proposition 187 will be the first giant stride in ultimately ending the ILLEGAL ALIEN invasion. It has been estimated that ILLEGAL ALIENS are costing taxpayers in excess of five billion dollars a year. While our own citizens and legal residents go wanting, those who choose to enter our country ILLEGALLY get royal treatment at the expense of the California taxpayer" (State of California 1994: 54; emphasis in the original).

As George Foster (1972) brilliantly noted in his famous essay "The Anatomy of Envy," in an ethos of "limited good" where somebody's gain (in this case immigrants) is framed as occurring at somebody else's expense (in this case citizens), envy becomes a dominant interpersonal concern. Framing immigration as a zero-sum issue ("their gain is our loss") can only fuel righteous anger. As Patrick Buchanan, the self-appointed culture warrior of American *fin de siècle* politics, said in a 1995 speech announcing his presidential candidacy, "Every year millions of undocumented aliens break our laws, cross our borders, and *demand* social benefits paid for with the tax dollars of American citizens. California is being bankrupted. Texas, Florida and Arizona are begging Washington to do its duty and defend the states as the Constitution requires. . . . Yet our leaders, timid and fearful of being called names, do nothing" (quoted in the *Boston Globe*, March 20, 1995; emphasis in original).

It is, of course, far from settled that undocumented immigrants are bankrupting California, costing the state "in excess of 5 billion dollars a year" as proponents of Proposition 187 claimed (see Passel 1994). But invoking the parasitic Other is of strategic importance in eliciting fury. In the language of Proposition 187, "while our own . . . go wanting [the immigrants] get royal treatment." Constructing the debate as a simple—and simplistic—they-win–we-lose proposition becomes a building block in the angry landscapes of Otherness now dominating public discourse.

These formations, I argue, deeply affect the children of immigrants. How do the children of immigrants respond to such assaults on their identity? We have proposed three Weberian ideal types to explore the range of experience among the children of Latino immigrants. Some second-generation youths raised in a context of ethnic conflict and disparagement may struggle to synthesize aspects of the two traditions. Among those who are successful and "make it" in the idioms of the dominant society, sometimes issues of guilt become important. In some such cases, particularly when one's success is experienced in the context of the deprivation and suffering of loved ones, feelings of guilt may be assuaged by helping less fortunate members of one's own group.

Rubén Navarrette, Jr.'s recent autobiography (1993) illustrates this pattern. When he came to see the enormous success that took him from a dusty California town to Harvard Square as having resulted in part from the failures of the Chicano classmates he left behind, Navarrette became overwhelmed with feelings of guilt and made a resolution to dedicate his efforts to help Latino students in rural California.

In our second ideal type we find those who may "identify" with the dominant culture and reject their own ethnic group (often called "passing"). Those who choose this route often have unresolved issues of shame and doubt for which they may struggle to overcompensate, as in the case of Richard Rodríguez (1982).

In our third type we find those who resolutely reject the society that rejects them and turn to those sharing their predicament—their peers. From this third situation typically emerge countercultural groups such as gangs rejecting aspects of the dominant society—including schools—and affirming their own ethnic identity (Vigil 1988).

Among Latinos, poor achievement in school continues to be a serious problem (Suárez-Orozco and Suárez-Orozco 1995). According to 1993 Bureau of the Census data, only 51.3 percent of all Latinos aged 25 and older completed high school (compared with 79.9 percent of all "whites"), and only 9.7 percent of all Latinos aged 25 and older completed four years of college or more (compared to 22.0 percent of all "whites"). Likewise, in Europe among the children of immigrants from North Africa the school dropout rate is alarmingly high.

In the United States there is a paradox that remains to be explored: according to an increasing number of studies, new immigrants from Mexico and Latin America in general display an eagerness to do well in school that is truly moving. Yet the longer Latino-origin youths are in the United States, the more skeptical many become toward school.

In our interviews recently arrived Latino youths told us of how they dreamed of achieving a career using the educational system to better themselves and the lot of their relatives. Likewise, teachers working with immigrant students in conflict-ridden inner-city schools largely reported their joy in seeing the positive energy and drive to learn among recently arrived Mexican immigrant students. These same teachers seemed perplexed telling us that the longer these immigrant kids are in schools, the more they become "like American students" (i.e., "disrespectful," "unmotivated," and even "cynical" in their attitudes toward school). Teachers told us that too many U.S.-born Latino students are not respectful and eager to achieve in the same way as their immigrant peers are.

Our research—along with a number of other studies—suggests that the Latino experience subverts the predictions of "assimilation" models that claim that in the United States each new generation tends to do substantially better than the previous one, eventually reaching parity with the mainstream population (see Portes 1996, Rumbaut and Cornelius 1995). U.S.-born Latinos continue to leave schools at alarmingly high rates. Among those who stay in school, Portes and his colleagues found in their exhaustive survey that recent immigrants tend to have *higher* GPAs than their U.S.-born peers. Likewise, Kao and Tienda (1995), working with the first panel of the National Educational Longitudinal Study of 1988 that selected a sample of 24,599 students from 1,052 randomly selected schools, found that immigrant students were more likely to express aspirations to graduate from college than third-generation U.S.-born students. Other studies suggest that third-generation U.S.-born

Latinos lag far behind whites in educational levels and occupational status. For example, Frank Bean and his associates found that

> [as Latino] immigrants and their offspring become more aware of the obstacles they face in further socioeconomic advancement, the second generation may not put as much emphasis on the further educational attainment of their children. . . . [And] the educational gap between third generation Mexicans and non-Hispanic white natives is not narrowing [which] provides discouraging news concerning the prospects for future assimilation. . . . The proportions of second and third generation Mexican American males who have completed less than twelve years of schooling are similar to one another, and both are much higher than those for non-Hispanic whites. (Bean et al. 1994: 91–92)

A number of studies suggest that too many second- and third-generation Mexican American youths are giving up on schools. We relate these findings to the vicissitudes in the path from immigration into minority status. Typically, immigrants endure their affective losses by concentrating on the material gains to be made by exploiting the new opportunities in a host country.

Members of the second generation, on the other hand, do not measure their current state in terms of life back in the old country. Rather, they use as their standard the ideals and expectations of the dominant society (Suárez-Orozco and Suárez-Orozco 1995). Using this standard, many children of Latino immigrants may fall short of their aspirations. Racism, disparagement, and lack of equal opportunity may compromise the faith of "at-risk" youths in their ability to make it. This may well be related to the disturbingly high school dropout rates among second- and third-generation Mexican American youths (Bean et al. 1994).

The findings of some of our recent studies are relevant when we take into consideration Ogbu's contention that "in general American social scientists . . . tend to assume explicitly or implicitly that the main cause of school failure lies in the background of the children" (1974: 3). By "background," Ogbu is referring to genetic, linguistic, psychological, and sociocultural characteristics. In the case of Latinos, and more specifically Mexican-origin populations, some have argued that cultural background is somehow responsible for the relatively high levels of school failure and dropout.

The empirical findings of our recent fieldwork do not support these contentions. Our findings suggest that the Mexican cultural background does indeed emphasize self-initiated achievement as well as the notion that hard work is critical for success, although Mexican American students value interdependence, familism, and obtaining help from others more than do white American students.

While our data reveal that Mexican youths in Mexico and Mexican immigrants maintain the conviction that school is the key to a better future, among more acculturated Latinos, we found a pattern of diminished expectations. It seems as though the more acculturated students are, the more skeptical and ambivalent they become about schools. In many ways the concerns of Mexican American youths oscillate between those of Mexican students and those of white American students.

These findings suggest that the problems in the motivational dynamics and schooling experiences of second-generation Latino youths cannot be attributed to cultural background per se. We must conclude, then, that a shift seems to occur in the psychosocial patterning of achievement motivation of Latino-origin populations *after* moving into minority status in the United States. Mexican American students may be assimilating to an American adolescent paradigm of ambivalence toward authority and schools. In addition, other factors, such as the stresses of minority status, discrimination, alienating schools, economic hardships, and pressures to work, may all contribute to the high dropout rate in this population. Further studies will be required to carefully examine the nature of this generational discontinuity.

The new immigration seems to be generating isomorphic conditions in varied settings. Although the new immigrants are needed in certain sectors of the economy, they have also been singled out with particular fury to account for all kinds of evil—from economic decline to crime epidemics. The new arrivals are disparaged by ethnic stereotypes characterizing them as lazy, parasitic, and crime prone.

Such disparagement has particularly poisonous effects on the children of immigrants. During adolescence the children of immigrants must struggle with special issues in developing a sense of identity while navigating sometimes conflicting cultural currents. In some cases, a reaction to psychosocial violence is to reject the institutions of the society that rejects them and to create "countercultural" identities. This may take the form of identifying with gangs and developing ambivalent attitudes toward the institutions of the dominant culture—including schools and authorities.

This majority-minority dialectic seems to have little to do with the culture of origin of a given minority group. It appears to occur in the second and third generations among diverse groups in various post-industrial settings. It is happening among disparaged second-generation Moroccans in Brussels, Turks in Germany, Koreans in Japan, and Latinos in the United States.

A number of studies—including some of our own—confirm what many teachers already know. Immigrants bring a special energy and optimism, perhaps to compensate for all the losses and mourning in migration, which is quite positive—when well harnessed. Study after study show that recent arrivals, whether they are Punjabi Sikhs in California, Hmong in Minnesota, or Japanese in Chicago (De Vos 1973), display achievement patterns which often surpass those of their native-born peers. Kao and Tienda's (1995) study of 24,599 eighth-graders concludes that immigrants and the children of immigrants perform better in school—receive better grades, score higher on standardized tests, and aspire to college at a greater rate—than their third-generation peers. Latino immigrants fit this pattern. Our work suggests that immigrants want to learn and want to work hard in order to achieve the dream of a better tomorrow—while maintaining a separate sense of identity.

However, the psychosocial violence, discrimination, and obstacles immigrants encounter affect the identity of many youths. This is particularly marked in the second generation. Throughout U.S. history, different ethnic groups have been the targets of different forms of debasement. Though arguably all experienced prejudice, all did not experience the same stereotypes. Previous waves of immigrants all had to contend with discrimination and hostilities. However, some groups are especially singled out for disparagement.

Latinos—along with African Americans in some respects—have had to contend with very insidious and destructive stereotypes. Furthermore, ongoing waves of new arrivals from Latin America invigorate old stereotypes. These stereotypes have been particularly devastating for adolescents, whose main task is to develop a positive sense of who they are. The images of Latinos reproduced in the media, in the teacher's lounge, in books, and now in the ballot box, include reference to crime-prone parasites, undeservingly feeding off American wealth.

The future of the world—and of the United States in it—is one of new forms of transnationalism, interdependence, and diversity. It is the challenge of the *fin de siècle* to creatively navigate—and attempt to resolve—the tensions, paradoxes, and contradictions these newly emerging social formations are engendering.

References

Bean, F. D., J. Chapa, R. Berg, and K. Sowards. 1994. "Educational and Socio-demographic Incorporation among Hispanic Immigrants to the United States." In B. Edmonston and J. Passel, eds., *Immigration and Ethnicity: The Integration of America's Newest Arrivals.* Washington, D.C.: Urban Institute, pp. 73–100.

Borjas, G. 1994. "Tired, Poor, on Welfare." In N. Mills, ed., *Arguing Immigration.* New York: Simon & Schuster, pp. 76–80.

Brinkley, J. 1994. "California's Woes on Aliens Appear Largely Self-Inflicted." *New York Times.* October 15.

Chávez, Linda. 1994. "Immigration Politics." In N. Mills, ed., *Arguing Immigration.* New York: Simon & Schuster, pp. 31–36.

Chávez, Lydia. 1994. "More Mexicans, More Profits." *New York Times.* December 9.

Cornelius, W. A. 1993. "Neo-Nativists Feed on Myopic Fears." *Los Angeles Times.* July 12.

Cornelius, W. A., P. L. Martin, and J. F. Hollifield. 1994. *Controlling Immigration: A Global Perspective.* Stanford, Calif.: Stanford University Press.

DeVos, G. 1973. *Socialization for Achievement: Essays on the Cultural Psychology of the Japanese.* Berkeley: University of California Press.

———. 1992. *Social Cohesion and Alienation: Minorities in the United States and Japan.* Boulder, Colo.: Westview Press.

Dollard, J., L. Dood, N. Miller, O. Mower, and R. Sears. 1939. *Frustration and Aggression.* New Haven, Conn.: Yale University Press.

Espenshade, T., and K. Hempstead. 1996. "Contemporary American Attitudes toward U.S. Immigration." *International Migration Review* 30 (2): 535–570.

Feldman, P., and J. Rainey. 1994. "Parts of Prop. 187 Blocked by Judge." *Los Angeles Times.* November 17.

Feldman, P., and P. J. McDonnell. 1994. "Prop. 187 Sponsors Swept Up in National Whirlwind." *Los Angeles Times.* November 14.

Fierman, J. 1994. "Is Immigration Hurting the U.S.?" In N. Mills, ed., *Arguing Immigration.* New York: Simon & Schuster, pp. 67–75.

Foster, G. M. 1972. "The Anatomy of Envy: A Study in Symbolic Behavior." *Current Anthropology* 13: 165–202.

Francese, P. 1994. "Aging America Needs Foreign Blood." In N. Mills, ed., *Arguing Immigration.* New York: Simon & Schuster, pp. 85–89.

Freud, S. 1930. *Civilization and Its Discontents.* Trans. and ed. by J. Strachey. New York: Norton.

Glazer, N. 1994. "The Closing Door." In N. Mills, ed., *Arguing Immigration.* New York: Simon & Schuster, pp. 37–47.

Golden, T. 1996. "If Immigrants Lose U.S. Aid, Local Budgets May Feel Pain." *New York Times.* July 29.

Hoffman, E. 1989. *Lost in Translation: A Life in a New Language.* New York: Dutton.

Horowitz, R. 1983. *Honor and the American Dream: Culture and Identity in a Chicano Community.* New Brunswick, N.J.: Rutgers University Press.

Huddle, D. 1993. *The Costs of Immigration.* Houston: Carrying Capacity Network.

Kao, G., and M. Tienda. 1995. "Optimism and Achievement: The Educational Performance of Immigrant Youth." *Social Science Quarterly* 76 (1): 1–19.

Klein, M., and J. Riviere. 1964. *Love, Hate, and Reparation.* New York: Norton.

Kohut, H. 1972. "Thoughts on Narcissism and Narcissistic Rage." *Psychoanalytic Study of the Child* 27 (1): 360–400.

Kristeva, J. 1991. *Strangers to Ourselves.* New York: Columbia University Press.

LeVine, R. 1966. *Dreams and Deeds: Achievement Motivation in Nigeria.* Chicago: University of Chicago Press.

McDonnell, P. J. 1994. "Complex Family Ties Tangle Simple Premise of Prop. 187." *Los Angeles Times.* November 20.

Meissner, D. 1992. "Managing Migrations." *Foreign Policy* 86 (4): 66–83.

Miles, J. 1994. "Blacks vs. Browns." In N. Mills, ed., *Arguing Immigration.* New York: Simon & Schuster, pp. 101–142.

Mills, N. 1994. "Introduction." In N. Mills, ed., *Arguing Immigration.* New York: Simon & Schuster, pp. 11–27.

Mitchell, S. 1993. "Aggression and the Endangered Self." *Psychoanalytic Quarterly* 62 (2): 351–382.

Navarrette, R., Jr. 1993. *A Darker Shade of Crimson: Odyssey of a Harvard Chicano.* New York: Bantam Books.

Noble, K. 1994. "California Immigration Measure Faces Rocky Legal Path." *New York Times.* November 11.

Ogbu, J. 1974. *The Next Generation: An Ethnography of Education in an Urban Neighborhood.* New York: Academic Press.

Passel, J. 1994. *Immigrants and Taxes: A Reappraisal of Huddle's "The Costs of Immigrants."* Washington, D.C.: Urban Institute.

Portes, A. 1996. "Growing Up American." Paper presented at the AAAS Annual Meeting, Baltimore, February 8–13.

Rodríguez, R. 1982. *Hunger of Memory: The Education of Richard Rodríguez.* New York: Bantam Books.

Rogler, L., D. Cortés, and R. Malgady. 1991. "Acculturation and Mental Health Status among Hispanics." *American Psychologist* 46 (6): 585–597.

Roosens, E. 1989. *Creating Ethnicity: The Process of Ethnogenesis.* Newbury Park, Calif.: Sage.

Rothstein, R. 1994. "Immigration Dilemmas." In N. Mills, ed., *Arguing Immigration.* New York: Simon & Schuster, pp. 48–63.

Rumbaut, R. G., and W. A. Cornelius. 1995. "Educating California's Immigrant Children: Introduction and Overview." In R. G. Rumbaut and W. A. Cornelius, eds., *California's Immigrant Children: Theory, Research, and Implications for Educational Policy.* La Jolla, Calif.: Center for U.S.–Mexican Studies, pp. 1–16.

Sanger, D. 1995. "Mexico Crisis Seen Spurring Flow of Aliens." *New York Times*. January 18.

Santiago, E. 1994. *Cuando era puertorriqueña*. New York: Vintage Books.

Sears, D. 1995. Personal communication.

State of California. 1994. *Proposition 187. Illegal Aliens. Ineligibility for Public Services. Verification and Reporting. Initiative Status.* Sacramento: State of California.

Suárez-Orozco, C., and M. M. Suárez-Orozco. 1995. *Transformations: Immigration, Family Life, and Achievement Motivation among Latino Adolescents.* Stanford, Calif.: Stanford University Press.

Suárez-Orozco, M. M. 1994. "Anxious Neighbors: Belgium and Its Immigrant Minorities." In W. A. Cornelius, P. L. Martin, and J. F. Hollifield, eds., *Controlling Immigration: A Global Perspective.* Stanford, Calif.: Stanford University Press, pp. 237–268.

———. 1996a. "California Dreaming: Proposition 187 and the Cultural Psychology of Racial and Ethnic Exclusion." *Anthropology and Education Quarterly* 27 (2): 151–167.

———. 1996b. "Unwelcome Mats." *Harvard Magazine*. July–August.

Vigil, J. D. 1988. *Barrio Gangs: Street Life and Identity in Southern California.* Austin: University of Texas Press.

Waldinger, R. 1994. "Black/Immigrant Competition Reassessed: New Evidence From Los Angeles." Unpublished manuscript. Department of Sociology, University of California, Los Angeles.

Wolf, D. 1988. *Undocumented Aliens and Crime: The Case of San Diego County.* La Jolla, Calif.: Center for U.S.–Mexican Studies, University of California, San Diego.

11

Potentially Traumatic Events among Unaccompanied Migrant Children from Central America

Ximena Urrutia-Rojas and Néstor Rodríguez

Political and economic turmoil caused severe hardships for many Central American children in the 1980s. In El Salvador, Guatemala, Nicaragua, and Honduras, rural and urban children aged seventeen and younger daily faced political violence and economic misery (Acker 1986). Instances of political violence included kidnappings, torture, the murder of family members and friends and of the children themselves, and widespread intimidation by armed groups (see Manz 1988, Benjamin 1987, Montgomery 1982). For many children as young as twelve years, political violence also included forced recruitment by combatant groups. Economic misery included family displacement from home, poverty, hunger, and homelessness. With about half of the Central American population under the age of twenty, the social plight of many Central American children was a major dimension of the turbulent Central American drama in the 1980s.

Facing overwhelming conditions, children were a major part of the massive emigration that characterized many Central American communities in the 1980s. While many children migrated with their families, many other children migrated unaccompanied by adults, either alone or in small groups of children, often headed to the United States. They walked and sometimes hitched rides on highway vehicles and trains to cover the more than one thousand miles from their Central American countries to the United States. Attempting to enter the United States without visas, thousands of unaccompanied Central American migrant children younger than eighteen were arrested annually by border agents of the U.S. Immigration and Naturalization Service (INS). In the late 1980s, the INS apprehended from two to five thousand unaccompanied migrant children annually for attempting to enter the country without visas.[1] As occurs among adult undocumented migrants, undoubtedly a greater number of unaccompanied Central American children crossed into the United States to become part of the country's undocumented migrant population.

Having already experienced traumatic and stressful conditions in their home countries (Martin-Baro 1989), unaccompanied, undocumented Central American children navigated through many difficulties in their journey to the United States. The children faced beatings, rape, robberies, extortion, hunger, accidents, and health problems on the journey north. Victims of rape during the journey, some girls had to deal with unwanted pregnancies. Even after arriving in the United States, some unaccompanied Central American children continued to experience stressful conditions, including economic exploitation, hunger, homelessness, and physical assaults.

In spite of the general lessening of conflict in the Central American isthmus, children in several countries in the region continue to experience in the 1990s some of the same conditions that characterized the turbulent 1980s. Not surprisingly, the consequences are the same: sizable numbers of Central American children continue to make the long trek north unaccompanied by adults, facing adult-size challenges along the journey.[2]

In this chapter, we elaborate on the situation of unaccompanied, undocumented children by presenting the findings from a study of Central American children under INS detention in the Lower Rio Grande Valley of Texas and in Houston in 1990. The study was conducted with two goals in mind: to obtain a sociodemographic profile of unaccompanied, undocumented Central American children migrating to the United States and to explore conditions that may affect the mental health of these children.

The study and its findings are presented in this paper as follows. First, we describe the research methods and instruments used in the study. Second, we present a sociodemographic profile of unaccompanied, undocumented Central American children based on intake records of children detained by the INS in the Lower Rio Grande Valley of Texas. Third, we give the results of personal interviews with detained children to describe the children's experiences with potentially traumatic events. Finally, we conclude the paper with comments regarding the continuing significance of unaccompanied Central American migrant children and mental health issues in the 1990s.

Research Methods

The study used three sources of data. One source consisted of intake records kept in three detention centers in the Lower Rio Grande Valley of Texas and in a foster-care program in Houston. Intake records of 1,259 children detained in 1989 were gathered from the child detention centers in the Texas border towns of Los Fresnos, Mission, and Raymondville. The intake records were used to obtain information concerning age, gender, and country of origin. In addition, the list of intake records served as a sampling frame to draw a random sample of intake records to analyze such characteristics as education, health problems, reasons for migrating, the presence or absence of relatives in the United States, and whether relatives were awaiting the children's arrival.

Originally a sample of 450 records was randomly selected from the 1,259 records; however, only 210 records were selected because of problems with the computerized records in the border detention centers. The records were compiled into a data base with 50 randomly selected cases from the much smaller number of detained children in a Houston detention program, for a total sample size of 260 cases. Testing for necessary sample size for a .95 level of confidence, the sample of 260 cases is sufficient for the male and female subsamples but insufficient for the Salvadoran and Nicaraguan subsamples. However, given the small ranges of the children's sociodemographic characteristics, it is likely that the differences between our findings and the findings of a sample with a larger number of Salvadoran and Nicaraguan children are minimal.

Personal interviews with detained children in the Texas border detention centers and in the Houston program served as a second source of data. Bilingual researchers in the study interviewed 133 children to ask if they had experienced potentially traumatic events specified in a list of events. Children were selected for interviews through informed consent and voluntary participation. The instrument used in the personal interviews consisted of two parts. The first part contained sociodemographic questions; the second part contained checklists of potentially traumatic events. Sets of events were grouped for the three settings of the community of origin, the journey to the United States, and the United States. Events selected and listed for the three settings were derived from several sources: from the researchers' previous experiences with Central American migrants, from literature reviews of refugee populations, and from consultations with a clinical psychologist (Missid Ghanem) with experience in studies of posttraumatic stress disorder in Lebanon.

The checklists were constructed in Spanish, translated into English, and then back-translated into Spanish. After the checklists were pre-tested, they were used in 133 interviews with detained children. Of the 133 interviews, 113 were conducted in the border centers and 20 were conducted in Houston. The interviews ranged from forty-five minutes to an hour.

Finally, researchers in the project conducted interviews of 60 detained children in the border detention centers and in Houston to assess the existence of posttraumatic stress disorder (PTSD) symptoms. The instruments used in this component of the study were Spanish versions of the Minnesota Multiphasic Personality Inventory (MMPI), Terrance Keane's Mississippi Combat Scale, and a Quick Quiz devised by a researcher assisting in the study, Nathan Denny. These instruments were idiomatically and culturally adapted for the children in the study.

Only children from El Salvador, Guatemala, Honduras, and Nicaragua were included in the study because these countries of origin constituted the core of Central America's instability in the 1980s. Also, children from Belize, Costa Rica, and Panama accounted for only 1 percent of the unaccompanied Central American children detained by the INS in the Lower Rio Grande Valley in 1989.

Sociodemographic Characteristics

Analysis of the 1,295 records of detained children in 1989 and of the sample of 260 cases drawn from these records indicates similarities and differences among the unaccompanied Central American children who have been detained by the INS.

NATIONALITY, GENDER, AND AGE

The distribution by country of origin of the children detained by the INS in the Lower Rio Grande Valley in 1989 indicates that significant numbers of unaccompanied, undocumented children came from El Salvador, Guatemala, Honduras, and Nicaragua (table 11.1). Not surprisingly, El Salvador and Nicaragua, the Central American countries with the most instability in the late 1980s, accounted for the largest proportions of the detained children.

For specific countries the sex ratios of males to females among the detained children were as follows: El Salvador, 4.9; Guatemala, 7.1; Honduras, 5.2, and Nicaragua, 2.2. Guatemalan children thus had the most un-

Table 11.1. Unaccompanied Central American Children
Apprehended by the INS in the Lower Rio Grande Valley,
1989 (percentages)

	El Salvador	Guatemala	Honduras	Nicaragua	Total
Male	84	88	84	69	80
Female	17	12	17	31	20
n	(443)	(225)	(218)	(373)	(1,259)

Table 11.2. Cental American Children Apprehended by the
INS in the Lower Rio Grande Valley, by Age Distribution, 1989
(percentages)

	Age						
	12 & under	13	14	15	16	17	n
Male	58	82	87	80	79	83	80
Female	42	18	13	20	21	17	20
n	(72)	(33)	(70)	(219)	(398)	(467)	(1,259)

even sex ratio, while Nicaraguan children had the most even ratio. It is possible that social conditions in the countries of origin affect the male-to-female migration ratio, with variation specific to unique circumstances. For example, local community norms may be more accepting of young men than of young women migrating alone.

Ages of the detained children in 1989 ranged from one to seventeen years. Children in the age interval of 16–17 accounted for over two thirds (68.9 percent) of the detained children (table 11.2).

EDUCATION

In the sample of 230 detained children, drawn from the records of the 1,259 children detained in 1989, half of the children had six years or less of schooling. About a fourth of the sample (25.2 percent) had three years or less of schooling, and about another fourth (25.7 percent) had six

Table 11.3. Reported Health Problems of Central American
Children in INS Detention in the Lower Rio Grande Valley
and Houston, by Gender, 1989 (percentages)

	Reported Health Problems		
	Yes	No	*n*
Male	72	88	85
Female	28	12	15
n	(46)	(196)	(242)

years of schooling. Only 2.2 percent of the children in the sample had
completed secondary education (high school). Years of schooling among
the children did not vary significantly by country of origin or gender.

HEALTH PROBLEMS

Almost one fifth (19 percent) of the children in the sample described
having a health problem when they were processed into detention (table
11.3). The most often reported health problems were depression, infec-
tions, urinary tract problems, dental problems, and abdominal pain. Health
problems were recorded at a significantly higher percentage for females.
Four of the 38 females in the sample were pregnant. Health problems did
not differ significantly by country of origin.

REASONS FOR MIGRATING

The children in the sample gave various reasons for migrating to the
United States. The reasons given by the children can be grouped into
seven categories: political, economic, political and economic, family reunification, adventure, educational, and personal problems with family
or neighbors (table 11.4).

Dichotomizing the reasons for migrating into politically related (either completely or partially) and nonpolitically related reasons produced
distributions that differed significantly by country of origin and by gender (table 11.5). Males were 1.4 times more likely than females to give
politically related reasons for their migration. Salvadoran children were

more likely, and Honduran children less likely, to state a politically related reason for migrating to the United States.

Dichotomizing reasons for migrating into economic (completely or partially) and noneconomic reasons produced distributions that differed significantly by country of origin but not by gender (table 11.5). Honduran children were more likely, and Nicaraguan children less likely, to state economic reasons for migrating.

RELATIVES IN THE UNITED STATES

A large majority (82 percent) of the children in the sample reported having one or more relatives present in the United States. This proportion did differ significantly by country of origin, but not by age or gender (table 11.6). Nicaraguan children were more likely to report having relatives in the United States, and Guatemalan children were less likely. Over three fourths (77.8 percent) of the children reported that they had a family member expecting their arrival in the United States. This finding varied significantly by country of origin, but not by gender. Nicaraguan children were more likely, and Guatemalan children less likely, to be expected in the United States by family members.

Table 11.4. Reasons for Migrating to the United States, Central American Children in INS Detention in the Lower Rio Grande Valley and Houston, by Country of Origin and Gender, 1989 (percentages)

	Political (P)	Economic (E)	P & E	Family Reunification	Education	Other	*Total*	*n*
El Salvador	44	32	13	3	6	3	101	(79)
Guatemala	24	44	11	4	11	7	101	(46)
Honduras	14	53	12	12	10	0	101	(51)
Nicaragua	44	23	7	13	15	0	102	(62)
Total								(238)
Male	37	35	12	5	10	2	101	(204)
Female	15	44	3	24	9	6	101	(34)
Total								(238)

Table 11.5. Political/Nonpolitical and Economic/Noneconomic
Reasons for Migrating, by Nationality and Gender (percentages)

	Political	Non-political	Economic	Non-economic	*n*
El Salvador	57	43	44	56	(79)
Guatemala	35	65	54	46	(46)
Honduras	26	75	65	35	(51)
Nicaragua	50	50	29	71	(62)
Total					(238)
Male	49	52	47	53	(204)
Female	18	82	47	53	(34)
Total					(238)

Table 11.6. Children Reporting Having Relatives in the United
States, by Country of Origin and Gender (percentages)

	Relatives Present in the United States		
	Yes	No	*n*
El Salvador	87	13	(84)
Guatemala	62	38	(47)
Honduras	82	18	(49)
Nicaragua	91	9	(65)
Total			(245)
Male	80	20	(208)
Female	92	8	(37)
Total			(245)

DISCUSSION

The finding that the largest number of children migrated from El Salvador and Nicaragua is not surprising, since these two countries suffered the most instability in the 1980s. The two countries were heavily affected by war, in addition to economic problems common to most of the Central American isthmus. It is important to understand, however, that in addition to the underlying societal factors that stimulate migration there exist community-specific conditions that at times foster migration from Central America to the United States. One such specific condition is the development of migrant networks that connect Central American communities to settlement areas in the United States (Hagan 1994). Networks provide important information and other resources for migrating north from Central America. Yet it remains an empirical question as to whether Central American children use migrant networks in ways similar to the ways adults use them.

Children's migration may be a subprocess of family migration. This is strongly suggested by the finding that a large majority of children in the sample indicated they had family members in the United States and that these family members were expecting the children's arrival. Yet, for a significant proportion of children, the unaccompanied migration north did not have an intended family reunification. Some children migrated to the United States primarily to avoid life-threatening situations in their communities of origin.

Finally, the finding that males make up a large majority of the children in detention is probably related to the greater involvement of males in combat roles. Some male children had migrated to the United States as army deserters and others to avoid forced recruitment in combatant groups. As stated above, no doubt community norms also affected the sex-ratio differentials among the detained children. It is possible that a lower sex ratio may exist among the children who migrate in family units.

Potentially Traumatic Experiences

In this section we report the findings of personal interviews conducted with 133 Central American children to determine if they had experienced any of the potentially traumatic events listed in interview instruments. Three lists of potentially traumatic events were used in the interviews: one list for events experienced in the home country, a second list for events experienced during the migration, and a third list for events experienced after arriving in the United States.

EVENTS EXPERIENCED IN COMMUNITIES OF ORIGIN

The interviews concerning the children's direct experiences of potentially traumatic events in their communities of origin focused on the following events: having one's home damaged by attack, being wounded, having a family member or friend killed, being kidnapped, being sexually assaulted, having one's life threatened, having shot or killed someone, one's school being attacked, being forcibly recruited into a combatant group, being physically assaulted or tortured, being forcibly removed from an area, experiencing drastic socioeconomic change, being homeless, suffering hunger, and encountering dead bodies. During the war-troubled years of the 1980s in Central America, these events were common in many Central American communities, rural and urban alike.

The mean number of different (but not necessarily total) potentially stressful or traumatic events experienced by the interviewed children in the community of origin was 3.8. More than half of the children (53 percent) reported experiencing four or more different potentially stressful or traumatic events in their communities of origin. The number of different events did not vary significantly by gender or country of origin.

Some significant differences were encountered by country of origin and gender for specific events. Guatemalan children were more likely to have suffered a drastic socioeconomic change, to have experienced homelessness, and to have suffered from hunger. Nicaraguan children were more likely to have been wounded, Honduran children were more likely to have been forcibly recruited, and Salvadoran children were more likely to have encountered dead bodies in their communities of origin. Males were more likely than females to have been wounded, to have shot or killed someone, and to have been forcibly recruited into an armed group (table 11.7). Females were more likely to have had a family member killed or to have been forcibly displaced.

EVENTS EXPERIENCED IN THE JOURNEY
TO THE UNITED STATES

For undocumented migrants the journey to the United States can involve many obstacles and problems, including assaults, hunger, and robberies. A major challenge for adult migrants, the journey can be particularly difficult for unaccompanied migrant children. To determine what potentially traumatic events they experienced on the journey to the United States, we asked the 133 children in the sample if they had experienced the following events during the actual migration: being physically assaulted, being sexually assaulted, hunger, being robbed, serious health problems, being seriously threatened or kidnapped, problems with police, exploitation or abuse, separation from family, death of a family member or other serious accident, being in danger of being returned to one's country, and other.

The mean number of different potentially traumatic events experi-

Table 11.7. Specific Events Experienced by Children in Home
Country (percentages)

	El Salvador	Gua- temala	Hon- duras	Nica- ragua	Male	Female
House consid- erably damaged	31	14	9	21	21	21
Wounded	14	0	25	37	22	4
Family member killed	41	36	38	53	36	61
Kidnapped	9	5	0	16	9	0
Sexually assaulted	0	5	13	0	3	7
Seriously threatened	48	36	50	47	48	39
Having to kill or shoot someone	14	0	22	26	20	0
Attack on one's school	28	18	6	21	18	29
Forced recruitment	50	14	59	47	59	0
Physically assaulted or tortured	17	14	34	32	26	11
Forced displacement	17	9	13	26	12	29
Drastic change of SES	9	36	16	26	18	14
Homelessness	9	41	31	21	22	18
Hunger	29	64	34	32	37	32
Encounters with cadavers	67	50	38	47	56	50

enced by the sample of 133 children during the migration to the United States was 3.7. This number did not vary significantly by country of origin or gender, indicating that the unaccompanied journey to the United States was similarly hazardous for females and males across the different Central American nationalities. Significant differences by country of origin and gender were found for the different specific events reported by the children (table 11.8). Nicaraguan children were more likely than Salvadoran, Guatemalan, and Honduran children to have experienced hunger. Females were significantly more likely than males to experience sexual assaults, have problems with police, have serious health problems, and be in danger of being returned home.

Table 11.8. Specific Events Experienced by Children on Journey
to the United States (percentages)

	El Salvador	Gua-temala	Hon-duras	Nica-ragua	Male	Female
Physically assaulted	21	22	38	32	28	18
Sexually assaulted	7	4	6	0	3	14
Hunger	86	74	91	63	84	75
Robbed	53	48	59	58	57	46
Serious health problems	26	26	38	21	24	43
Seriously threat-ened or kidnapped	26	13	28	37	26	21
Problems with police	59	57	59	63	64	39
Exploited or abused	5	0	9	21	9	0
Separation from family	7	0	13	16	9	4
Serious accident	2	0	6	5	3	4
In danger of being returned to country	7	48	56	63	66	36
Other	5	4	18	11	11	4

EVENTS EXPERIENCED AFTER ENTERING THE UNITED STATES

Entering into the United States does not end the problems that undocumented migrants face in their journey. In the United States, undocumented migrants continue to face substantial risks, including being apprehended and deported by U.S. agencies. To determine what potentially traumatic events they experienced after entering the United States, we asked the 133 children in the sample if they had experienced the following events: being physically assaulted, being sexually assaulted, being seriously threatened, being maltreated or abused, being in fear of being deported, hunger, vagrancy, being previously detained by government agents, being deported, being in fear of legal proceedings regarding their undocumented status, being in fear of integrating with family, prostitution, exploitation, and unemployment.

The mean number of different potentially traumatic events experienced by the children after arriving in the United States was 2.3. This mean value did not vary significantly by country of origin or gender. Significant differences by country of origin and gender were found for two of the listed specific events (table 11.9). Nicaraguan children were more likely than other Central American children to have experienced hunger, and female children were more likely than male children to have been previously detained.

The mean number of total different potentially traumatic events experienced by the children was 9.8 and did not vary significantly by country of origin or gender. On the average a child reported having experienced a total of about ten different potentially traumatic events in the settings of the community of origin, the journey to the United States, and the United States. Almost three fourths (74 percent) of the interviewed sample of children experienced from five to fifteen total different events.

Table 11.9. Specific Events Experienced by Children after Entering the United States (percentages)

	El Salvador	Gua- temala	Hon- duras	Nica- ragua	Male	Female
Physically assaulted	8	0	3	11	7	0
Sexually assaulted	4	0	3	0	2	4
Seriously threatened	6	5	7	6	7	1
Maltreated or abused	9	5	7	1	7	4
Fear of being deported	64	71	83	67	71	67
Hunger	15	24	50	28	31	15
Vagrancy	15	24	30	33	26	15
Previously detained	18	24	17	0	19	4
Previously deported	11	14	7	0	10	7
Fear of legal procedures	25	33	40	28	30	33
Fear of inte- grating with family	4	5	13	11	7	7
Exploitation	6	0	7	6	4	7
Unemployment	21	38	40	28	40	26
Other	11	24	13	6	13	15

DISCUSSION

The findings of the children's experiences with potentially traumatic events indicate that Salvadoran, Guatemalan, Honduran, and Nicaraguan children faced similar stressful and potentially traumatic environments in their home countries and in their journeys to the United States. Yet significant differences occurred in the type of event experienced by gender and to some extent by country of origin.

The finding that the mean number of different potentially traumatic events experienced in the home country and in the journey were almost identical indicates that for the unaccompanied migrant children the migration process itself is as hazardous as being in their troubled home countries. Unaccompanied migration thus becomes another source of stress and potential trauma.

The findings of similar levels of experiences with different potentially traumatic events may be affected by the way the interview instrument was constructed. The instrument contained broad categories of potentially traumatic events, without adjusting the categories to specific characteristics. For example, for the question "Was your home seriously damaged [in military conflict]?" the responses were not coded by the specific manner of damage—for example, by fire or by aerial bombardment. It is possible that this type of specificity may influence the potential psychological impact of the event.

Overall, the findings of the children's experiences of potentially traumatic events indicate that the unaccompanied children faced major problems at all stages of their migration process. The significance of this situation is twofold: a large majority of the children had experiences of *several or many* potentially traumatic events, and a large majority of the children had experiences of *different* potentially traumatic events. Even after reaching the United States, the children were not safe from potentially traumatic experiences. As an examination for PTSD symptoms revealed, for some children these experiences did create conditions of serious anxiety disorder (Rodríguez and Urrutia-Rojas 1990). Using a Spanish version of the PTSD scale of the MMPI, seven of sixty children assessed for anxiety disorder scored at or above the PTSD cutoff score. Using a Spanish version of the Mississippi Combat Related PTSD Scale, six of the sixty children scored at or above the PTSD cutoff score. A total of eleven children (18.3 percent) scored at or above the cutoffs established for PTSD on one or both scales. The PTSD scores for both scales were found to have statistically significant correlations with the sum of potentially traumatic events experienced in the journey to the United States, but not with the sum of events experienced in the home country or after entering the United States. The use of a third PTSD assessment scale, the Quick Quiz scale devised by a project researcher, found significant correlations between PTSD symptoms and events experienced in the home country and in the journey to the United States.

Conclusion

Political and economic problems in Central America took a heavy toll on the children of the isthmus during the 1980s, especially in peasant and working-class communities. Many children in these communities experienced the wrath of war and the ravages of economic deprivation. Their suffering was equal to the suffering experienced by children in Southeast Asia, Africa, the Middle East, and other troubled world regions. Caught in an international drama of U.S. geopolitics, however, most Central American children who emigrated unaccompanied by adults received little support from the government of the country to which they turned for refuge. The very journey to the United States turned into a highly risky and injurious experience equal in severity to conditions in their troubled homelands.

Many more unaccompanied Central American children enter the United States annually than are apprehended by the U.S. government. Over the years since the 1980s, these children amount to a substantial population contributing to the growth of the young adult Central American population in the United States. It is important, therefore, for community agencies and institutions in the United States to seriously consider the situation of Central American immigrant children in the country. Agencies and institutions working with Central American immigrant children should take into consideration the children's experiences of potentially traumatic events. The findings of several anxiety disorder symptoms among the children in our study indicate that Central American children have a need for programs and services to deal with mental health problems they may be experiencing. This need will not disappear in the near future, since persisting political and economic problems in Central America will continue to cause the migration of unaccompanied children from the isthmus to the United States.

Notes

1. We obtained this range of apprehensions from conversations with INS officials.

2. Unaccompanied Central American children continue to appear in large numbers in established centers for Latino immigrants and refugees in various U.S. areas, such as Houston and the Lower Rio Grande Valley.

References

Acker, A. 1986. *Children of the Volcano.* Westport, Conn.: Lawrence Hill.

Benjamin, M., ed. 1987. *Don't Be Afraid, Gringo: A Honduran Woman Speaks from the Heart.* San Francisco: Food First, Institute for Food and Development Policy.

Hagan, J. M. 1994. *Deciding to Be Legal: A Maya Community in Houston.* Philadelphia: Temple University Press.

Manz, B. 1988. *Refugees of a Hidden War: The Aftermath of Counterinsurgency in Guatemala.* Albany: State University of New York Press.

Martin-Baro, I. 1989. "Political Violence and War as Causes of Psychological Trauma in El Salvador." *Journal of La Raza Studies* 2: 5–13.

Montgomery, T. S. 1982. *Revolution in El Salvador: Origins and Evolution.* Boulder, Colo.: Westview Press.

Rodríguez, N. P., and X. Urrutia-Rojas. 1990. "Undocumented and Unaccompanied: A Mental-Health Study of Unaccompanied Immigrant Children from Central America." Working paper 90-4. Houston: Institute for Higher Education Law and Governance, University of Houston.

About the Contributors

Paula Acevedo Cantero received her bachelor's degree in biology from the Autonomous University of Madrid (UAM) and also has a master's degree in anthropology. She is a researcher at the Unit of Physical Anthropology (Department of Biology) at UAM. Her main concerns are nutrition and women's biology.

Sophie Alexander, M.D., Ph.D., is an obstetrician and gynecologist. She is a researcher in perinatal epidemiology at the School of Public Health of the Free University of Brussels, Belgium.

Redouane Ben Driss is a psychologist-therapist at the Centrum voor Welzijnszorg (Center for Mental Health) in Brussels. The center specializes in medical anthropology and cross-cultural therapy with immigrants, asylum seekers, and political refugees. He has studied the identity of North African adolescents living in Belgium. He has participated in the foundation of organizations for immigrants and heads several study groups on the mental health of immigrants.

Pierre Buekens, M.D., Ph.D., was trained in obstetrics and gynecology before becoming involved in perinatal epidemiology. He is the chair of the Maternal and Child Health Department at the University of North Carolina at Chapel Hill's School of Public Health.

Thérèse Delvaux, M.D., M.P.H., is an obstetrician and gynecologist and has extensive experience working in Africa and Asia. She is a researcher at the School of Public Health of the Free University of Brussels, Belgium.

Aimé De Muynck, M.D., Ph.D., is a professor of epidemiology and head of the Department of Epidemiology at the Institute of Tropical Medicine, Antwerp. Since 1983 he has been actively involved in research on the health and health care demands of Moroccan and Turkish migrants, as well as on the quality of care provided to them. He was the founder and first president of the Center for Ethnic Minorities and Health.

Antoine Gailly is a psychologist-anthropologist and the director of the Centrum voor Welzijnszorg (Center for Mental Health) in Brussels. The center specializes in medical anthropology and cross-cultural psychotherapy and works with immigrants, asylum seekers, and political refugees. He has done research in Turkey and on Turkish immigration in Europe. Gailly has published several articles on Turkish culture, medical anthropology, and cross-cultural therapy in national and international journals. He is a member of the European Platform on Multicultural Societies and Mental Health.

Francesca Gany, M.D. (Mount Sinai School of Medicine), M.S. (Graduate School of Public Service, New York University), is an assistant professor at the New York University School of Medicine, where she teaches internal medicine, immigrant health, and health policy and medical economics. She is the founder and director of the New York Task Force on Immigrant Health, a network of health practitioners, social scientists, community advocates, and policy makers dedicated to improving the health status of New York's immigrants.

Isabelle Godin, Dr. P.H., is a sociologist with a strong research background in minority health issues. She is a researcher at the School of Public Health of the Free University of Brussels, Belgium.

Esperanza Gutiérrez Redomero, Ph.D., is a biologist and associate professor at the University of Alcalá Henares (Madrid), where she teaches human ecology. Her research interests are the bioanthropology of maternity and perinatality and the relation between social environment and birth defects.

Fred Louckx holds a Ph.D. in sociology and is a professor of medical sociology. He is the head of the Section of Medical-Social Sciences at the Free University of Brussels and the chairman of the Society and Health Resource Center, which specializes in such areas as socioeconomic health differences and unequal access to health care. His other fields of interest include ethnic minorities and health and the study of sentinel health events in rehabilitation centers.

María Dolores Marrodán Serrano has a Ph.D. in biology from the Universidad Complutense de Madrid, where she is a professor of physical anthropology. Her field of interest within human ecology includes human growth and development, nutrition, the anthropology of sports, and reproductive models.

Godelieve Masuy-Stroobant, Ph.D., is a demographer with the Belgian National Fund for Scientific Research and a member of the faculty at the Institute of Demography of the Catholic University of Louvain in Louvain-la-Neuve, Belgium.

Yolanda C. Padilla is an assistant professor in the School of Social Work at the University of Texas at Austin. She holds a Ph.D. in social work and sociology from the University of Michigan. Her research focuses on the study of the socioeconomic status of Mexicans in the United States, including the impact of immigration, and on comparative ethnographic analyses of poverty conditions on the U.S.–Mexico border and the implications for social service delivery.

Consuelo Prado Martínez holds a Ph.D. in biological sciences from the Autonomous University of Madrid. She is a professor of physical anthropology at the College of Sciences at the same university. Her main area of interest is the study of women, and she has researched reproductive behavior, nutrition, and human growth and development.

Lars Rasmussen holds a B.A. in economics and government from Beloit College, Wisconsin, a master's degree in economics from the London School of Economics and Political Science, and a Certificat des Études Superiures es Sciences Politiques from the Graduate Institute for International Studies in Geneva, Switzerland. He also studied at the Institut d'Études Politiques in Paris and at the University of Copenhagen, where he has taught philosophy of social sciences. At present, he is principal administrator at the Public Health Directorate of the European Commission with special interests in aging and health.

Néstor Rodríguez is an associate professor in sociology and director of the Center for Immigration Research at the University of Houston. His research and publications focus on undocumented immigration, transnational communities, intergroup relations between new immigrants and established residents, and urban development. He is currently participating in a study of the social, cultural, and economic linkages between the metropolitan areas of Houston and Monterrey.

Ángeles Sánchez-Andrés holds a Ph.D. in biology from Alcalá de Henares University, where she is a professor of physical anthropology. Her fields of interest include child growth and development, as well as genetics. She studies the inheritability of morphophysiological characteristics and corporal composition.

Julia Sebastián Herranz, who holds a Ph.D. in psychology, is professor of psychobiology at the Autonomous University of Madrid. Her research interests include the causes of depression and the portrayals of women by the media.

Marcelo M. Suárez-Orozco is a professor of human development at Harvard University. In 1996 he was appointed the Norbert Elias Lecturer at the Amsterdam School for Social Sciences. Suárez-Orozco is the author of many works on immigration and cultural psychology. His most recent book, *Transformations: Immigration, Family Life, and Achievement Motivation among Latino Adolescents,* coauthored with Carola Suárez-Orozco, won the 1996 Social Policy Award of the Society for Research on Adolescents.

Heike Thiel de Bocanegra, M.A. (Psychology, University of Bielefeld, Germany), M.P.H. (University of North Carolina at Chapel Hill), has worked for six years in public health and community development programs in Peru. She taught courses at the Pontificia Universidad Católica del Perú and the Universidad Femenina in Lima. Since 1991, she has been a project director and member of the Executive Advisory Committee for the New York Task Force on Immigrant Health (New York University School of Medicine).

Ximena Urrutia-Rojas, R.N., holds a Ph.D. in public health from the University of Texas, Houston. She has conducted research on health and access to health among U.S. Latino and immigrant groups in the Lower Rio Grande Valley of Texas and in the Houston area. She has published papers on health and access to public health services among new Latino immigrants and on the immigration and settlement conditions of Central Americans in Texas in the 1980s. She is currently a research associate at the Center for Immigration Research at the University of Houston.

Hans Verrept has studied philology and cultural and social anthropology. He is a research assistant at the Free University of Brussels and at the School of Family Medicine at the University of Antwerp. His main field of interest is the development of strategies to improve the quality of health care delivered to ethnic minorities. He is currently working on a project that has as its aim the development of a system for ethnic monitoring in health care in Belgium.

About the Editors

Gilberto Cárdenas, Ph.D. (University of Notre Dame, Indiana), is an associate professor of sociology at the University of Texas at Austin and the executive director of the Inter-University Program for Latino Research, which is a consortium of Latino research centers in the United States. From 1991 to 1996 he was director of the Center for Mexican American Studies at the University of Texas at Austin. His areas of interest include international migration and ethnic studies.

Antonio Ugalde, Ph.D. (Stanford University), is a professor of sociology at the University of Texas at Austin and coordinator of the Human Rights and International Migration Project. He is also an adjunct professor at the School of Public Health of the University of Texas, Health Science Center, Houston. He has been a visiting professor at the Andalusian School of Public Health (Granada, Spain), at the University of Pittsburgh, and at the Department of Social Medicine, Universidad del Valle (Cali, Colombia). His fields of interest include social change and development and political sociology.

CMAS BOOKS

Health and Social Services among International Labor Migrants: A Comparative Perspective was designed by Jace Graf and Víctor J. Guerra. The text was composed primarily in Minion, with Hiroshige used for the title page and chapter titles. The book was printed and bound by Edwards Brothers, of Ann Arbor, Michigan.